Find Your PERFECT Partner

Wayne C. Allen

2012

© 2012 Wayne C. Allen, M.Th.

The Phoenix Centre Press
55 Northfield Drive, Suite 324
Waterloo, Ontario, Canada 2K 3T6

email: waynecallen@gmail.com
website: http://www.phoenixcentre.com

Library and Archives Canada Cataloguing in Publication

Allen, Wayne Charles, 1951 –

Find Your Perfect Partner
ISBN 978-0-9877192-1-8

1. Zen 2. Self Actualization

All rights reserved. No part of this book may be reproduced or utilized in any form, or by any means, mechanical or electronic, including photocopying, recording or by any information storage or retrieval system, without written permission from the publisher.

Disclaimer

The contents of this book are solely the opinion of the author and should not be considered as a form of therapy, advice, direction and/or diagnosis or treatment of any kind: medical, spiritual, mental or other. If expert advice or counseling is needed, services of a competent professional should be sought. The author and the Publisher assume no responsibility or liability and specifically disclaim any warranty, express or implied, as regards this book. The purchaser or reader assumes responsibility for the use of this book.

Dedication

To Darbella MacNaughton, who walks with me, holds me, teaches me about grace, and loves me as I am.

Other books by Wayne C. Allen

Also available on Amazon as Paperbacks, and for Kindle:

Half Asleep in the Buddha Hall

Wayne's "Eastern" book takes you by the hand and leads you to Zen-based peace of mind. *Half Asleep in the Buddha Hall* is a Zen based guide to living life fully and deeply. Using Zen stories old and new, as well as other illustrations and exercises, Wayne C. Allen takes you on an adventure into the uncharted territory of yourself.

This Endless Moment

Worthwhile change comes at a price. If you're tired of the same old relationships, the same situations cropping up again and again, and you find yourself stuck in the middle, then right now, you can do something about it! It's time to decide!

If you are willing to commit to living the life you have dreamed of, surrounded by meaningful and deep relationships, while making a real difference in the world, you need *This Endless Moment*.

Contents

Introduction 1
Chapter One - Finding Ourselves First 3
Chapter Two – Lives on the Edge 16
Chapter Three – The Basis of Relationships 28
Chapter Four – A Little Theory That Grew 34
Chapter Five – First Things First 45
Chapter Six – Who've You Had in the Past? 51
Chapter Seven – The Contents of a List of 50 58
Chapter Eight – Down to the Basics 76
Chapter Nine – Examining Your Language 80
Chapter Ten – Ordering the Cosmos 84
Chapter Eleven – Be a Poster Poster 87
Chapter Twelve – The Big Question 90
Chapter Thirteen – The Friend Factor 94
Chapter Fourteen – Why This Works 96
Chapter Fifteen – Some Closing Thoughts 102
The Forms 104
Comments about The List of 50 107
Other People's Lists 115
References 134

Introduction

In 1997 I created a company website[i] to describe the work we do at The Phoenix Centre, as well as to promote and sell my books. One of the suggestions was to provide free stuff.

I decided to offer three relationship booklets – two of the booklets were about building more elegant and functional relationships. The third booklet was *The List of 50*.

I wrote The List of 50 from personal experience.

I realized that the screwy relationships I had been in (prior to actually thinking about how to create an elegant one) were a direct result of *my* inattention.

Back in 1983, I made a clear decision about my "next" relationship. That year, I also finished my counselling degree and met Darbella, (or Dar for short – an amazing woman who brooks no foolishness when it comes to relationships.)

My self-realizations led me to devise a rudimentary *List of 50* for myself. More on the *List of 50* below!

Many years have passed since I wrote the initial booklet, and I find that I am frustrating myself. I notice that most relationships these days - simply and plainly - suck.

The divorce rate in the US and Canada is abysmal. As for the relationships that do not end in divorce, I am not seeing a ton of contentment and real relating. It is painfully clear that, of all committed relationships, perhaps 5 percent to 10 percent are successful.

And, it's getting worse.

So much tension, so much distrust. And really, although I might be accused of over-simplifying, the vast majority of the confusion in relationships has to do with one or both of the participants trying to *change the other into the person they wish they had actually married.*

I decided to re-write the booklet, and to say much more about the place of *rational thought* and *conscious awareness* in the establishment and maintenance of relationships.

Pretending the important, life-altering decision to relate is "a matter of the heart" is not only stupid, it is *not working.*

This book, then, is a guidebook for finding your perfect partner. You'll discover the tools you need to figure out the kind of person you want to be in relationship with.

The plot is simple: I'll write about what goes wrong in relationships, and especially how you need to establish a set of *filters.* The *filter set* is: what I am looking for in a partner.

We'll look at how most of us relate, and explore common beliefs that get in the way of great relating. Then, we'll move into the meat of this book: creating a *List of 50.* The *List* is a well thought out guide to the kind of person you want to share your life with.

Finally, we'll explore making the *List* work, by resetting your brain to discover people who fit your *List.* And I'll even tell you why all of this works!

Let's get to it!

---

[i] http://www.phoenixcentre.com/

Chapter One - Finding Ourselves First

Life is not as it is. Life is as you are.

While I am sure you'd like to rush right along to the "good stuff" about how to find your perfect partner, please stick with me here. I can guarantee that the points you are about to read are essential for your future relationship happiness.

Let's start with an exploration of what doesn't work.

Likely you're reading this because you know that something isn't quite right about your understandings regarding:

- how relationships form,
- what attracts or repels you, and
- how cultural myths about relationships are actually your worst enemies.

If you live in the west, you are bombarded with endless piles of crap about relationships.

Movies, TV, book, magazines – all are invested in shoveling it deep and wide. Most people never consider what happens to movie couples "after the credits roll." Movies tend to end at the "... and they lived happily ever after" stage, and viewers never get to see the effort involved in maintaining a relationship.

Here's the problem: we are programmed into believing that good relationships "should" just happen, almost spontaneously. You know the drill.

Your eyes drift across a crowded room, and lock on to Mr. or Ms. "Right." The vibes travel back and forth, and as the orchestra plays, you walk (in slow motion) toward your "perfect life," which of course is filled with unending bliss.

That no one has ever actually experienced the start of a successful relationship this way never occurs to us.

Typically, relationships "tank" when the novelty of "hormones" wears off - at that point, we start *judging*.

First of all, we judge that the other person is flawed.

We think that they were keeping their real nature a secret, and that we were lied to. Time went by and the 'real' person suddenly appeared.

We judge that the other person did not love us as we deserved. (Of course, we also believe that the other person has nothing better to do than to love us the way we want to be loved, 24/7...)

We are conditioned to look outside of ourselves for validation, happiness, and direction.

Now, western society would collapse if people stopped looking "outside" for their satisfaction – stopped buying what is being sold. But the western approach is based on "never good enough."

No matter how "good" something is, in order to keep us buying, the marketers have to convince us that we need a *better* version. We are jaded – we are convinced that satisfaction comes from outside of ourselves.

If you are 'normal,' you've been conditioned to think that others should behave in a certain way – that the people in your life *should* want to make you happy. The problem with this view is that it simply does not work.

It does not work because all such a belief creates is two people making demands on each other - what you want and you need vs. what your partner wants and needs - coupled with the idea that others should put you first. I think you see the problem - when both do this, there has to be a conflict.

Now, objectively, how would we determine which of these mutually exclusive needs "should" be fulfilled? In other words, what makes what *you* want more important than what *your partner* wants?

Yet, in most relationships, love is equated with obedience. Because of this, in your failed relationships, you endlessly judged that the other person was not "treating you right." You were unhappy, and you blamed your partner.

In this book, I am talking to you, and only you.

I will ask you who you are, and encourage you to self-explore - to figure out what is going on for you, and thus to let go of making *yourself* unhappy.

I think your key task is getting to know and accept all sides of you. When you accept and love yourself, you will not need affirmations and confirmation from your partner (you won't be 'needy.')

You will be free to clearly choose who to be in relationship with – based on the characteristics that are important to you – not based upon their willingness to endlessly prop you up.

The only thing that matters in relationship is:

"Am I learning about myself in this relationship? Do I make myself happy in this relationship? Is my partner the person I primarily want to share myself with – body, mind and spirit? Do I feel encouraged in my walk, and is my partner a person I can open up to unconditionally?"

It's not about convenience, nor about keeping your partner around so you will not be scared or afraid, and it is not about making life easy. Life is not easy, nor is being in relationship easy.

Here are a few other beliefs you will need to let go of:

The Myth of One Reality

The Myth of One Reality is this: there is only one way of understanding things - one answer, one explanation. Of course, by some mysterious process, the "one reality" is always the one you already perceive and hold.

We really do know, in our heart of hearts, that the "one reality, forever" view just does not hold water over time. For example, recent advances in science have overthrown many cherished beliefs. And as we look in the mirror as years go by, we see how much our bodies change.

Nonetheless, we still crave "endless sameness."

Most couples who come in for relationship therapy want me to declare his or her view of the relationship as "the one *true* reality" - each wants me to side with them against their partner.

They hate it when I say that in almost all cases there are two (or more) sides to everything, and that nothing is absolutely true.

Accepting the relativity of truth is a scary proposition.

It means that I will have to understand that my truth – my reality – is what I believe, in this moment. My reality will only *imperfectly* match the reality of another person.

As a social convention, we agree to agree, but this is more an exercise in semantics than "the truth."

There is also a cultural assumption about relationships - that there is one "right way" for couples to be.

I hear couples saying, "Here's what *we* should be doing." I have the worst time convincing them that they are individuals. It is especially difficult to get people to recognize that their perspective is not *right* - it is simply their *perspective*.

You need to learn that elegant relating is not about determining right and wrong. It's only the question of *utility* - does this perspective work (get me what I say I am looking for)?

The Myth of Comfort

The Myth of Comfort says that nothing should be painful. There should be no lessons, other than easy ones.

We of the 1950s and later grew up under the Myth of Comfort, Security and "Having it Better than Dad." Do you remember annual raises? People got them because that was what happened each year. Our *right*, we thought. Now, we whine because raises might never come, or come because of performance or some actual quality standard.

Personal growth was the buzzword of the 1960s. It, too, was to be easy and quick. One *est* weekend here, one colonic there, a chant and a mantra and everything would be different.

When anyone suggested that enlightenment came in fits and starts, after much effort, and with painful self-knowledge and continual effort, the Cult of Comfort said, "If I give you more money, can you speed up the process?"

These days, many cocoon in their Lazy Boys, hoping that their pain will stop. They figure, "It wasn't supposed to be this way."

Well, baloney. As Scott Peck reminded us in *The Road Less Traveled*, (Peck, M. Scott, pg. 15) "Life is difficult." Learning, changing, and healing - all comes at a price.

In fact, no learning happens without pain. The pain may be nothing more than the stress of having to give something - some behaviour - up, or it may be a "shaken to the foundations" type of pain, but it is a necessary component of growth.

Despite intuitively knowing this, many wish it were different. Most people are stuck in one or more of the following comfort beliefs:

Happy versus Right

Many folk want to be *right*. It is not required that the other person change - the "fun" is in judging others *wrong*. Wanting to be *right* requires little of the person – as being *right* never involves self-reflection. It simply involves finding people to judge and declaring them to be lacking.

Happiness is inversely proportional to judging. The more you judge others, the less happy you are. The wise person learns that the first and greatest discipline is to focus on simply observing others, rather than judging them.

Manipulating others into changing so you don't have to

This one goes, "If only you would see the pain you are causing me, and if you really loved me, you would change."

This is otherwise known as guilting.

We want to be able to blame others for our distress. It is easy to blame, harder to take total and complete responsibility for the things that are happening in our lives.

Because of the Cult of Comfort, we think our partners should have our best interest in mind. It is quite a shock to discover they do not. Many people solve this problem by changing partners. The brave few simply recognize that wholeness is not about getting others to do what we want them to.

"I'm no good"

I have a client who regularly bursts into tears and says, "It's my fault. I am not a good person. I'm to blame." This is not as bad as it seems, as at least she is using the right pronoun - it is her life and is all about her.

It is also a "stuck in the Comfort Zone" technique.

Her feeling bad about herself is simply a habit, just like every other dysfunctional behaviour. It requires no effort, because people who use such lines never finish their thought by saying - "... and so here is what I am going to do differently."

This technique allows you to sit back, tell yourself off, feel bad, sulk, maybe get some attention from those around you, and not have to change a thing.

The Myth of Comfort vanishes when we adopt the "truth of wholeness": You are responsible for your life, and only you can change the way you see your life. Only you can change the way you respond to others and treat yourself. You are response-able - able to respond.

The Myth of Dreamland - Past and Future

There are three *frames* for living out our lives - the past, the present, and the future. The whole person chooses which frame, which dream-state, to live in.

The present is not true! It is simply where we are, at any given time. Choosing to live in the Here and Now is *always* subjective. This reflects back to the Myth of one Reality, but we need to push it further.

You are never being objective! We filter everything and everyone through our prejudices. Yes, we all have them. Just think of any sort of person you cannot stand. I am not asking you to question the prejudice (which I call a *filter*), just to recognize its existence. You dislike this person because of the way you choose to filter your experience.

We can never say much more than, "This is my present understanding, which may change." Admitting we may not know something "for sure, forever" is a real stretch for many people. On the other hand, at least we are telling the truth by admitting that we do not know the truth.

One reason for choosing to live in the present is that this is where life is actually happening. Now, this is obvious, right? That does not, however, keep most people from spending much of their waking time in their heads, re-examining the past and thinking about the future.

This is not to say either activity is wrong, in and of itself. We remember the past so we can learn from it. I, for one, do not want to have to learn repeatedly not to put my hand on the glowing red coil on my stove. We remember in order to have a base of experience - experience helps us to sort out the present and make logical choices about it.

We also need to future-plan, while recognizing that such planning is *provisional*. Things change. We want to remember that just because we planned something, and therefore expect it to turn out as planned, there is no guarantee that it will turn out that way. We practice, we focus, and we head off, as prepared as possible, into an unknown future.

Contrast that to what people usually do. Most people visit the past in order to remember past failures, insults, sicknesses, distresses, and rejections. They play the movie in their heads, watch the train wreck, and feel bad.

Then, they flip to the future and see all sorts of grim catastrophes coming because of their poor past choices. Paralyzed between the past and the future, they create a mind-space where nothing in the present changes.

Now, it takes some work, but I often am able to convince my clients that their recollections of the past are not very reliable, as their experiences have passed through their filters. In other words, most couples construct a past to fit their preconceived notions of each other and themselves. They actually miss any contrary data.

It may be hard to face, but there is no *truth* to our versions of the past. This is why, for example, siblings fight with each other and with their parents over descriptions of past events. You hear two or more versions of the same incident. Why? Because everyone saw it differently - each saw it through his or her prejudices and beliefs about their place in the family - through their filters.

How would a wise person ever figure out which version was true?

All you should care about is whether your view is helpful.

The Myth of Limitations

Much like the rest of the myths, limitations are self-imposed, and usually for no good reason. Now, I am not talking about jumping off a ten story building and thinking I am going to land safely. I am talking about what we tell ourselves about our relationships, our skills and talents, our bodies and our minds.

Years ago, as a kid, I learned from a very wise person that I should determine *for myself* who I was and how I would act. If I listened to the opinions of all the people around me, I would be running from one thing to the next, trying to be everything to everyone.

Limitations are artificial constructs. By believing in them, you get to whine along with everyone else. I guess it is true: misery really does love company.

In our view, to believe that we are limitless - that we can chose to create, achieve, and really make a difference - this is the mark of wholeness. This is the mark of life well lived.

I would suggest that you take a moment from your reading, and note down anything that has occurred to you regarding your own limiting behaviours. Have I touched any nerves in the last few sections? What myths do you believe in?

Strange Behaviours to Notice

Here are several behaviours that many engage in, yet lead precisely nowhere:

Blaming

Scott Peck, in *The Road Less Traveled*, (pg. 35) differentiates between neurotics and persons with character disorders this way - neurotics blame themselves, and those with character disorders blame everyone else. He wrote that he would rather work with a room full of neurotics than one character disordered person. Why?

The neurotic person is right. The stuff we have to deal with *is* our responsibility. We are not to blame, until we know better. Then, I am not above asking how many times a person has to bash into the wall before noticing it is there.

Blaming *others* is a linchpin of our society. If you listen to the news, you will be bombarded with the blame flavour of the month. Used to be the Russians. Then Iran. Now it is Iraq and radical Islamism. Of course, all the jobs are going to immigrants. On and on.

Grown up kids blame their parents - for everything. "It's not my fault. I can't do anything about it. My parents failed me." This was the principal *whine* of the latter part of the 20th century - and it is continuing and deepening in the 21st.

We hear this "blame game" so much that it becomes our world-view. When something goes wrong, rather than turning inside and wondering how we set life up to go the way it is going, we look around for someone to point a finger at.

The problem with this, of course, is that it means that nothing will change. It will not change because the person doing the blaming is looking for a solution outside of him or herself.

Inertia

Another behaviour that is common and useless. Inertia is *choosing* to stay stuck. Inertia happens as we decide there is nothing we can do about our lives, our problems, and the world. It is a cousin to giving up (see below), but not quite so passive.

Cocooning is the modern equivalent of inertia. You turn your home into a fortress designed to protect you from the outside world. You line it with comfortable things, and make all your connections outside through media - the Internet, through e-mail, through television. You surround yourself with sound - noise. You sit in the middle of it all and tell yourself you deserve it - you work so hard.

Boredom

Another cousin. This is *intellectual* cocooning. Your brain shuts off. Life seems monotonous and dull. You place the blame on "the world" for not being stimulating enough. Alternatively, you assume that the people around you are boring. A key expression is, "We just don't have fun anymore."

We thus reduce *people* to *objects*. We judge people on their ability to amuse us. People become disposable, as we look for an emotional *charge*. Yet, at our depth, we know we will not find it. Boredom excludes the possibility of change.

Giving Up

This is the end of the trail, and is just short of clinical depression. At this point, you assume not only that nothing will change, but also that nothing *can* change. You believe that society is sliding down a slippery slope to oblivion.

Causes that seemed important now seem irrelevant. Relationships seem meaningless. There is no *purpose*.

The Way Out

Well, enough of the rant about what *does not* work. Let's begin our exploration of what *does* work. The key is a shift of focus - from living life as a helpless observer to living life awake and aware – on the *cutting edge*.

Chapter Two – Lives on the Edge

Like it or not, finding peace and contentment in life, and elegance in our relating, is determined, *exclusively*, by the choices we make. Or, to use precise language,

"My life is determined by the choices I continue to make."

The choice to live life on the edge is an interesting one. To make this choice, I have to focus my entire being on staying conscious and paying attention. It is the equivalent of walking a tightrope. Lose focus, snooze, you lose. To walk on the cutting edge is possible; lose focus and you are going to be cut.

Five elements form the basis for living a fulfilled and meaningful life. They are:

Creativity

Tension

Focus

Commitment, and

Choosing the Growing Edge

Creativity

Creativity is the ability to take any situation, old or new, and to devise several alternative responses to the situation. Another term for creativity is lateral thinking - stepping out of the predictable is a valuable skill.

If there is a major fault with how people come to *maturity*, it is in how deliberately society conditions creativity out of our children.

We see it, for example, in the reaction of a parent to their child's painting. Often, we hear, "That's a lovely painting, but grass is green and the sky is blue, and people aren't purple. And the house needs a roof and the dog needs one less leg."

Now it just may be that the child actually perceives the world exactly as she paints it. She may be seeing auras around people and the aura may be a brilliant purple. Maybe she is seeing the earth in the sky and the sky mixed into the earth. Maybe dogs run so fast that they seem to have five legs, and maybe the house is her heart, looking to be as open as it can be.

Suzie may survive until school. If she keeps on painting what her *inner eye* of creativity sees, she will be corrected, graded down, and finally, some brilliant teacher will say, "Suzie, you're a really neat kid, but you'll never be an artist."

We teach our kids to regurgitate *facts*. Even when we teach kids to figure out how they learned something in the first place, we give little attention to creativity.

Now, lest you think this is an unimportant topic, do a little research and find out how many companies hire *consultants* to come in and teach their employees creative thinking. Other names are lateral thinking, innovation, right brained thinking, but the plot is the same.

The company has hit the wall, is stagnant, and is failing. They have tried making the employees work harder, they have fired some people to get the bottom line in balance, and they may have even *considered* their customers.

However, all that has happened is that the present employees, doing variations of the same thing, keep reinventing the same broken company.

Enter creativity specialists. Often, it is when we stop trying to *solve problems* and instead *empower people to be creative*, that a new path opens up.

So, exactly what is creativity?

"Creativity is placing something on a pedestal and walking all around it."

Most people, when confronting an issue - their lives, money, relationships, profit and loss – have learned one way (a two dimensional way) of looking at the situation. All other possibilities are filtered out. It is not that there are no other possibilities. Other options are available, but not noticed.

Filters are necessary, but abused in the extreme.

A filter is a device used to limit the transmission of something. For example, a blue filter "filters out" all colours of light except blue.

Similarly, the mind has a series of filters to remove irrelevant data from the endless stream of input. These filters are sub or unconscious.

Let's talk about how filters are used. Brain scientists know that we are bombarded with thousands of messages per second. You can get a sense of this by imagining: you are on the expressway, driving. You are off in la-la land, and drive past your exit. You curse; you wonder, "Where did I drift off to?"

Now, same situation, but this time, a truck driver slams on the brakes, right in front of you. You swerve left into the open lane. You were as much in la-la land as in the other example. Your brain, however, was sub-consciously watching the traffic. Your inattentive butt is saved again, despite the fact that you were unaware (unconscious of) what was happening.

Once you get this idea, it is not difficult to apply it to the reactions we have to events and interactions. In most cases, we learned one or two ways of doing things.

Usually, we learned to do what those before us did. This is limiting in the extreme, and doing the same thing repeatedly, while expecting a different result is a classic definition of insanity. (That was a joke, sort of.) The way out is creativity.

Back to the concept of creativity and the pedestal

My point is that we tend to deal with our lives in two dimensions. We learned to reduce schoolwork (problems) to paper. When we imagine a person or a thing, we do the same.

We make our issues flat and two (or one) dimensional. We picture it in front us, and then snap in our filters (being a victim, never being listened to, whatever.) This behaviour gets us nowhere, and explains why we repeat behaviours that we tell ourselves we are *trying to change.*

When I was training to be a psychotherapist, a MSW student asked me to help her figure out her relationship.

Her boyfriend was from a German Lutheran family, and was studying to become a Minister. He wanted a wife that was dark-haired, stayed at home, and would "pop out" many little PKs (Parson's Kids.)

Find Your Perfect Partner

My MSW friend was blonde, dynamic, flirty, really into her career, and wanted to be childfree. She couldn't figure out why she was miserable about the relationship.

She had *worried about the relationship* for a long time before I came on the scene. She was (and here is **the filter** that was determining her choices) afraid to end the relationship, lest she never find a better fit.

In her two-dimensional way, she saw a picture of her boyfriend, realized that there was a fundamental conflict, and froze. Her fear kept her from exploring options – she got no further than hoping, "Maybe he'll change once I marry him!"

She knew I did hypnosis, so she asked for help. I helped her go into a trance, and led her through *The Pedestal Exercise*.

I had her place her boyfriend up on a pedestal, walk all around him, look at him from all angles, and *really see him*. That is all I said. I let her have that experience for five minutes, and then I ended the trance.

When she got home, she thought of him again. He appeared in three dimensions, back on the pedestal. Her eyes snapped open. She raced into the bathroom and threw up. She then called him and dumped him.

As soon as we tell our minds that an issue is three-dimensional, we tell ourselves that there are an infinite number of ways of seeing that issue. Immediately, the two-dimensional filter drops away, and we begin to generate *new ways* of being and doing. Our ineffective rules fall away.

Now, at the end of the day, we *may* re-impose the old ways of relating to the object, person, or issue. What is new is that we will do so by choice, and for a "real" reason. (We will do it because we have chosen, not because, "That's the way I always did it.")

More than likely, though, *nothing* will be the same. We will find ourselves stunned by the number of possibilities for dealing with our issue in new, exciting ways.

Then, we will actually have to do something.

To continue the story of the blonde MSW student - summer break came. The next fall, I was driving on the campus. I saw my client's best friend, standing with an attractive dark brown-haired woman. I stopped to say hello.

Upon closer examination, *I realized that the brown-haired woman was my blonde MSW friend.*

We talked. She had run into her ex-boyfriend, and out of desperation, decided to see if she could fix her misery by changing *herself*.

She decided to finish her degree, marry him, quit her profession before it began, and follow him into his Ministry, having babies as they went along. The process began with a bottle of hair dye, dressing conservatively, and reining herself in.

This is the opposite of "He'll change." She surrendered her "self" to his demands. Another two-dimensional "fix" to a three-dimensional problem.

Footnote: You may be relieved to know that I met her again a decade later. She was blonde again, a practicing social worker, dating, and had dumped Herr Pastor after six months.

It is not enough to see clearly, three-dimensionally. It is not even enough to put your understandings out there, in words. You can list them, post them on the wall, tell your therapist, your friends, and your significant other. If you do not actually implement your new thinking, you, by default, will fall back into the familiar.

You have to be committed to *living your creativity* – after you see things differently, you must change your behaviour.

Creativity, then, is a pedestal upon which to build wholeness. You understand that there is no *best way* to do anything. If we can couple constant improvement to our way of seeing, we are as close as we will ever be to the truth of what works.

To do so means we have to be willing to embrace both uncertainty and change.

Tension

Tension is the energetic feeling of *charge* that occurs when how things are and how I want them to be is not equal. The tension regulates itself as I accept the inevitability of tension, and work toward upping my tolerance for change.

OK. So what? Well, doesn't it strike you that most people are not looking for a balance between competing forces, but rather are looking for no tension at all?

Remember, back when you were a kid, when you tried something new and it did not work out, and someone said, "See? Better to leave well enough alone!" Most of us have received that message at some point in our lives. "Don't rock the boat." "Don't make an example of yourself." "Don't call attention to yourself." Or my personal favourite, "You made your bed, now lie in it."

Our upbringing was all about socialization, and that means behaving in a predictable way, regardless of whether the way we live, the way we are, is much less than who we can be.

Change, for most, is scary

Few people make peace with change. Those that do are the non-conformists, the free thinkers – in short, the people who choose not to settle for the status quo.

Far from running from tension, they *create* tension. They are willing to challenge everything. They look for the improved way. They recognize that there is no good, nor bad. There is just stuck (what doesn't work) and not stuck (what works).

Rocking the boat has led to the invention of everything you see. Refusing to leave well enough alone has led to every profound change humankind has ever made. Tension is the moment that exists in time and space between what is, and what can be.

Tension exists because someone chooses to propose an alternative, to wiggle the system, to look at life differently. It is asking, "Why not?"

Focus

Focus is bringing one's full attention to the issue at hand, using past experience as a resource, while future-pacing probable outcomes. Focus means "living in the moment."

Focus is the bedmate of tension. As we propose new ways of seeing, everything on earth will try to distract us. Most people react negatively when others change. No matter how well they understand the vision, the direction, the motivation for change, the idea that they, personally, will have to change sends them reeling.

And then, they decide to reel *you* in.

Of course, we do this to ourselves, too. We discover a pattern in need of change, a better way to communicate, an innovative project, and then the self-doubts start. We list all the reasons the change cannot happen, (or who else has to change before change will happen,) and we slam on the brakes.

Focus is about staying with a project, direction, or exercise – staying with this book! – until the project is completed. Focus is the ability to be aware of all of the negativity about the project, both from without and from within, and moving forward with it anyway.

It is not supposed to be easy. If it were easy, you would have done it already. Once you learn how to focus, you will wonder why it took you so long.

Then, the next new thing will emerge, and suddenly it is difficult again. However, you will have learned, and you will push forward.

Focus is about where we choose to direct our attention. It is not about getting everyone else to agree that we should focus. It is about single-minded focus geared at creating growth and change. No matter what is going on around you.

Commitment

Let's think for a minute about what we are committed to. Most people tend to commit to *stuff*. To causes. To people. To jobs. To making money or collecting toys. Especially, people commit to their worldview and to their self-view.

We thus become experts at self-justification. We see things a certain way, and we commit ourselves to making that way of seeing things absolute. Depending on our energy level, we may try to convert the world.

Of course, we conveniently forget that nothing in the world (inside or outside) stays the same, so we face the impossible contradiction of trying to be committed to something that is changing.

We pretend that the thing that is changing is not changing.

You hear, for example, a person describing her husband's flaws. She will invariably say, "He's *always* like that." Well, of course he isn't. He's a fluid process, not a fixed thing.

Go ahead. Pretend that you can commit to something. Imagine committing to your job, a political party, or religion. Now, walk with me. Step back. How secure is your job? How stable is your party? How loving and caring, how intelligent, is your religion?

You will likely go in two different directions here. The first voice will jump up and defend what you have committed to. There will be, though, in the background, a little voice, saying, "Well, it isn't perfect, or secure, or much of anything. However, I have put so much energy into it! I can't imagine giving up on it, just because it doesn't work."

Believe it or not, you're half way there.

Let me try a radical thought. What if, instead of committing to a series of things, you commit to *only one principle*? And that one principle is this:

"*I commit to staying awake while examining my life.*"

Interesting. Socrates once said, "The unexamined life is not worth living." Most do not examine their lives. Most examine the things their lives contain.

Commitment to understanding how and who we are, at this given moment, is a key to developing healthy and whole relationships and a dynamic persona.

Commitment to *stuff*, on the other hand, leads precisely nowhere, simply because such a commitment means we never think we have enough. Not enough of the person we are committed to. Not enough toys.

To commit as I suggest changes everything.

Using the "understanding myself in relation to" model, you ask yourself, "Given the present situation with the person I'm dating, how am I? Am I responding in a way that deepens our relationship?"

You no longer feel compelled to judge the other person (and, of course, find them lacking!) You simply reflect on yourself and see where you are. From there, it is a relatively short walk to changing what needs changing (in yourself) and celebrating what works.

Choosing the Growing Edge

Growing edge: The place where drama, tension, and disagreements coalesce.

We tend to try to avoid growing edges because there is pain there. Because of our avoidance, the issue is ignored or papered over. With attention, the growing edge becomes a vehicle for transformation.

The wise soul seeks guidance for walking through the pain.

I worked with a young man whose life changed after a motorcycle accident (he was driving) that claimed the life of his best friend. For 11 months, he struggled to understand "Why this happened to me." Finally, he shifted his thinking. Rather than seeking to understand, he allowed himself to feel his loss, claim his responsibility, and began the healing process.

He accepted that **healing hurts**, but also realized that he felt *relief*. This is how as it should be.

Growing edges are where the hurt is. If we do not go there continually, we will never have a hope of true healing. On the other hand, this is not a prescription to *only* be where there is hurt. It is a *non-avoidance* prescription. We know for sure the situation will not change until such visits take place.

The work is about going to the growing edge, dealing with *a piece*, and then moving away.

The body, when injured, does not focus *only* on the injury. There is air to breathe, blood to pump, infections to fight, hair to grow (for most of us), and things to see and hear. The body deals with the injury in the midst of life. As should we, as we touch our spiritual and emotional lives.

Chapter Three – The Basis of Relationships

Now that we've had a bit of a look at the foundations of human relating, we turn our attention to the meat and potatoes of this book. From here on, we'll be covering how people typically form relationships, why this doesn't work, and how to change this norm by applying what we call *The List of 50*.

You will be given examples and clear explanations, so you can experiment with what is contained here in the comfort of your own home.

Let us begin, then, at the beginning. Let us look at how relationships come to be, and what we can do to improve our odds for a great relationship.

Sex, Hormones and Horniness

Relationships begin with an initial triggering of pleasure hormones. The initial "sexual attraction" helps couples "find each other" – sexual attraction is the basis for almost all relationships.

Richard Dawkins, in *The Selfish Gene*, (p. 15) suggests that the

"selfish part [of our behaviour and personality] is actually the genetic pull to replicate one's genetic patterning."

Thus, at a hard-wired, chromosomal level, the goal of life is DNA replication. The feeling of sexual attraction is caused by visual and scent cues that the person would make a good match for our DNA. The cues trigger an "attracted to" response.

For example, the hourglass figure prized by many males indicates good nutrition and a pelvis wide enough to give birth easily. The muscular torso and upright posture of a healthy male demonstrates a constitution rugged enough to provide for the family while keeping the wolves from the door. (Remember: we are talking about genetic predispositions and patterns here, and they are 100,000 generations old. The things that draw us to each other are ancient. They *do not line up with* modern sensibilities like the equality of the sexes.)

Most relationships follow a pattern.

I'll describe this from a male perspective to save torturing pronouns. Women are going through an identical process, with slightly different emphasis.

There is the initial observation phase. I already have a mental picture (a *filter*) of what I find attractive, so if I am attracted, the person has passed "pre-qualification."

I then pop into my head and start up the fantasy machine. I start to "guess" (based upon my fantasies, as I have no information) about the availability and desirability of the woman.

If my observations hit a nerve for me (literally and figuratively), I have a *genital-hormonal reaction*. A hard-wired, electro-chemical flush or reaction whispers to my cells, "Move forward, and chat her up."

Now, I may have spent a lot of time deciding about the characteristics of the person I want to be in relationship with. At the moment – this moment of "charge" – it does not matter!

Because my hormonal rush is such an overwhelming experience, my mind is being "trumped" by my hormones.

Sidebar: Interestingly, if I pay attention, I'll notice the *tension* I described in the last chapter. This is a warning sign that I'm shifting to auto-pilot. I can then *also* engage my brain!

In the first flush of meeting and getting turned on, our hormones attempt to convince us that the person we're lusting for would be "a perfect fit!" At the hormonal level, it is not about long-lasting, deep, and meaningful relationships.

It is about getting us to breed.

During the hormonal phase, if reason and thought fly out the window, there is little focus on the character, life direction, and life purpose of our intended.

If we consider who the person is *at all*, we quickly decide that anything we don't like can be fixed by asking (and later demanding) that the person changes.

To recap, it is almost as if we are saying to ourselves, "Wow, she's cute. I really like her. I think I will ask her out. If there are other things about her I don't like, she'll change because she'll love me."

And thus the dance begins.

In the early dating stage, we are on our best behaviour. We read the other person carefully for signs and hints of what they want in a mate. We attempt to become that kind of person, to provide for their needs, even if it flies in the face of who we actually are.

After six months, the veneer begins to wear off. We start acting more normally; so does our partner. At this point, there is a *rush of disappointment.* A sense of being lied to.

That's when another dumb little internal voice kicks in and says, "Oh well, I've got six months invested in this relationship, and I may never get another chance, so I'm going to stick around anyway, and just try harder to change her."

After the Novelty Wears Off

From that point on, unless they wise up and cut it out, there will be an attempt by one or both persons to change the other person, to get the other person to behave, to force the other person to be someone they are not. As this is a no-win situation, most relationships continue, forever, to be a battle.

Or, the parties stop fighting and become apathetic. Or, the partners split.

I spend a lot of time with couples who have followed this path, and end up in my office, not at the first hint of trouble, but years into the relationship. They are looking for a way to stop fighting.

It is *possible* to help these couples to learn to respect each other as persons, and to teach them to develop excellent communication. However, the underlying reality for most of these couples, is this –

"She is not the person I should be in relationship with. I love her, but I do not particularly like her. I'm doing therapy to stop the fighting, make the best of the situation, and gain some energy to get on with the rest of my life."

This is a worthwhile and achievable goal. I make myself sad, however, as these couples will never know the joy of a deep and meaningful relationship.

A Small Explanation

I have been sitting with individuals and couples, discussing failed and marginal relationships, since I began training to be a therapist back in 1981. I have witnessed to so much pain and heartache and disappointment.

I sometimes have a moment of wishing I could turn back the clock for this person or that couple, and get in there at the six-month point, or even before they met. I want to reset their internal drives, so that their mindless pursuit of a partner stops being a desperate search for *anyone*.

I want to tell them that it is all right - they did not fail - they just did not know better.

It was because of all of the pain (theirs and mine!) that I came up with *The List of 50*.

Having just experienced my second (!!) failed marriage (this in 1983,) I was determined to discover why I, a highly intelligent and intuitive guy, had such a lousy track record with relationships.

I knew that hormones are always with us, and will act as a primary determinant for the kind of people to whom we are attracted. Nevertheless, I wondered, what would happen if people were also *intentional* and *practical* about deciding whom to be in relationship with?

What if they decided, in advance, about the communication style they wanted to have, and the life focus and direction their relationship would work from? What if they committed to engaging their brains alongside their hormones?

What came to me, "way back when," was that we get into weird relationships because we do not know, have never thought about, what we are looking for in a partner. We also haven't committed to waiting for a person who matches what we are looking for.

We are stunned to realize that the person we are with "happened to us" totally by chance.

We counteract this by resetting the *filters* for what kind of person we are seeking.

I developed *The List of 50* to counteract our reluctance to think about and actively plan for the relationships we will engage in. After years of working with this technique, both personally and with my clients, I have seen impressive results. I now share this concept with you.

In the next chapter, I want to tell you my personal experience with this idea.

Chapter Four – A Little Theory That Grew

There are three things you have to "get":

Self-responsibility: I am totally and completely responsible for me - for my actions, my thoughts, and my beliefs.

Self-knowing: My goal in life is to engage with myself and with others, in order to discover who I am today, and what my purpose is.

Elegant Relating: I choose to be completely honest, clear in my communication, and curious regarding the experiences of others.

Back in 1982, I was in the second year of a two-year Counselling Internship, a part of my masters' degree in counselling.

I knew there was some *concept* I was missing regarding how to build an authentic relationship.

One night, after spending a weekend studying hypnosis in Toronto, I decided to use a visualization to figure out what I was missing regarding elegant and intimate relating.

I asked my internal wise person the following question: "Why are so many people miserable in their relationships?"

I picture my wise person as an old guy with a wicked wit and sense of irony. He never gives me a straight answer to anything. (PS – If you'd like to create an internal wise person, download my free booklet, The Watcher.[ii])

This time, he gave me a picture in my head.

I saw two lines. I saw a long, long line of men, and a long, long line of women. The people in the lines were moving forward, slowly, eyes to the front. I looked at the front of the line, and watched.

As a male and a female reached the front of the line, they turned to each other, looked each other up and down, smiled, joined hands, and walked off into the sunset.

That was it.

My wise man said, "And thus it is with all relationships. Without forethought, it's the luck of the draw."

Later that evening, I played the image back.

The long, long lines represented the part of the population that did not "get it." This was how they picked the person they were going to spend the rest of their life with!

What it boils down to:

"Here I am in line, ready to meet the person I'm going to spend eternity with, and I'm willing to do that with **the next available person***."*

I later modified this to,

"If you don't put effort into which person you choose, you get to spend the rest of your life with **the next bozo in line***."*

Think about it. Think about relationships you have been in or the relationship you are in now. What were the characteristics you were looking for in the other person? If you are "normal," the characteristics were:

- the sex of the person,
- the appearance of the person,
- that s/he should be *fun* to be with, "into" the same things I am,

Find Your Perfect Partner

- that s/he comes from a *good* family,
- and will love me (meaning he/she will do what I want him/her to).

So, we end up with the next bozo in line.

Reason: all the aforementioned description gets you is a person of a particular sex who looks good to you. Characteristics like "fun to be with" and "into in the same things I am" are so vague as to be meaningless.

*Now, lest you think I figured any of this out **easily**, let me tell you a little bit about my relationship history. It's a quite good story about how all of this works, and I do not embarrass easily...*

I am, as of this writing (2012) into the 26th year of my *third* marriage. My partner, Darbella (Dar, for short) and I have the kind of relationship I wish for all people. Getting myself to her after working through where I'd gone off the rails in other relationships took me a while.

As this is Dar's first marriage, we jokingly say that she spent the twenty-eight years before she met me waiting for me to grow up and figure myself out.

My first marriage happened at the end of my first year in university, in 1969. This was the quintessential hippie wedding thing. We knew each other for a month, liked each other's "vibe," got married, and were divorced in 1971.

I returned to university in September of 1971, having resumed dating my high school sweetheart during summer vacation back home in Buffalo. Soon, it was January of 1972. I chose not to take courses that month, had some time on my hands, and wandered into the Campus Bookstore.

There, (pant, pant) right there at the cash register, stood the woman of my dreams (well, at least one of my dreams.)

Blonde, blue-eyed, 5'4", pretty, nice smile, and nice body (all according to me and my preferences…)

Please Note! This is the beginning and end of what I *actually knew about her*. I was simply having a hormonal reaction to a "type" that I find attractive.

Here comes the story-telling, the speculation – the justifications.

I decided that:

- she was smart (she was in College, so I assumed she was smart,) and
- industrious (she had a job in the book store,) and
- she liked me (she smiled at me and blushed a bit as we chatted in the line.)

Her name was "Sue." [Well, not really ;-)] She was studying to become a tech professional, and she said it was nice to have met me.

I wandered out of the Bookstore in a hormonal daze. I decided, in this order, that

- I wanted to sleep with her, and
- I wanted to date her.

I started a campaign to win her body and her mind.

By the end of January, I had accomplished both. In February, she moved in with me. We had fun, we talked, and we learned more about each other.

By May, I was scratching my head. She seemed to be into "stuff," into getting a good job that paid lots of money, and was not into politics or vocational thinking. I was studying to be a minister/therapist and was deeply into protesting the war in Viet Nam, fighting for civil rights, helping people, etc.

I found that I was often angering myself over things she said or did. Finally, I decided that enough was enough. I broke up with her, just before the Semester ended.

She moved out, we decided to remain friends, and I flew home to Buffalo, to the waiting arms of my former high school sweetheart.

At the end of August, while packing to go back to school, I suddenly realized that I needed a ride from O'Hare to good old Elmhurst College. Sue had a car. I called and asked if she would mind picking me up. She agreed. Off I flew to Chicago, anxious to get back to classes.

As I exited the O'Hare Airport baggage area, there was Sue, and the image is burned into my brain to this day.

Sue was smiling her dazzling smile. What caught my attention was her outfit - a miniscule blue halter-top and tight white short-shorts. Her long blonde hair was loose and cascading over her shoulders. I dropped my bag and just about stepped on my tongue.

She moved back into my dorm room that night.

Now, let me hasten to add that nothing about Sue had changed – except for her outfit. She later gleefully admitted spending an inordinate amount of time picking the outfit, and its entire purpose was to lure me back.

Right from square one I knew that nothing *fundamental* had changed. As the months went by, I knew that I was just putting in time. I would regularly end the relationship, taking time off to pursue other women. I knew I was looking for something I was not getting with Sue. I just did not know what it was.

And then, we'd get back together, for no apparent reason other than convenience and the sex.

I graduated in 1973 and went to work at a bank. More breaks in the relationship, as I dated around and moved up the ladder at the bank, while building a respectable photography business on the side.

In 1974, Sue went off to graduate school. Just prior to her leaving, we were sitting in my car, and were talking about the future. Interestingly, I only talked about my jobs and my vocation - about using the bank as a stepping-stone to doing counselling and consulting.

I never once said a word about Sue and me. It was as if I could not see a future with Sue.

I now know that I had *settled* for the relationship I had with her. I was not happy with much of it. There was still no meaningful communication (according to my way of looking at it) and we continued to have diametrically opposed views on how life might best be lived.

Leaving the relationship, however, seemed like too much effort, so I had decided simply to make the best of it. Our "What's going to happen in the future" conversation said it all: I was not interested in the relationship. I was interested in my vocation.

Sue said, with her most tremulous voice, "But what about us?" A little voice, deep inside, shouted, "Run!" (I have since learned to trust that voice...) My mouth said, "Well, after all this time, we probably should get married."

And, in 1975, we did.

I will fast-forward the clock to 1983 now. What I learned in the interim - in the actual living out of our lives - was that our life views were completely different.

Sue and I had our own views of what was crucial, and our crucial lists never lined up.

We tried counselling. I would list my issues, and Sue would say, "My marriage is perfect. I wouldn't change a thing." We entered counselling often, but never got past one session, as it is impossible for couple counselling to have a chance of working without at least half-hearted participation by both parties.

During my counselling internship, my therapist and supervisor would ask, "Why are you married to Sue?" I would reply, "Because I love her," and she would go, "Hmm."

In December of 1983, that question finally made sense.

I had led a particularly difficult meeting. During the meeting, a woman expressed hurts that went back years. No one had ever actually listened to her before. I gave her the space and support to say what she needed to say, even the angry parts, some of which she aimed at me.

We resolved her issues. She said, "Thanks for listening. I apologize for yelling at you." I said, with a wink, "That's OK. I never heard a word."

I would likely say that differently now, but I later checked with her and indeed, she heard what I intended - that I had not taken her yelling as *being mad at me*. I was glad to have provided an ear, and a sounding board, with no demand that she behave herself.

She had resolved her issue, and I was glad I had helped.

When I got home that night, I was full of beans. I told Sue what had happened. She promptly tried to hand me my head. She said I was cruel and insensitive, handled the situation badly, and besides, *I was late getting home.*

When she finished, in a flash of clarity, I realized that her speech, far from being about how I had treated the woman, was a scathing description of how Sue saw our relationship and me. My therapist's question now rang in my ears. I said, "The marriage is over." And it was.

I understood then, (and relearned it over the next months, as I grieved the death of my marriage) that my process had been what I described above. I got into the relationship with Sue on the basis of her looks, her being in college, and "the glint in her eye."

As I got to know her, I subconsciously realized that her personality and mine did not mesh, nor did our goals, nor our aspirations, nor our style of being in the world. Especially, our styles of communication were miles apart. In short, we were fundamentally (at the internal, hard-wired level) as different as two people could be.

So, I did the "normal" thing. I entered into an 11-year campaign to change her into the woman I wanted in my life.

My realization, back there in 1983, on the night the marriage ended, was that *there was nothing wrong with Sue.*

She was fine, perfect, just the way she was. I had absolutely no right to insist that she change to make me happy. (Never mind that she never changed even an iota. I kept trying.) I had spent a decade thinking I knew what was best for another person. That she successfully resisted my attempts says volumes about her strength.

I also realized that, if she found and married someone who had the same values she had, she would be much happier, and that the same would apply for me. (That is exactly what did happen.)

I decided I did not want to repeat this behaviour. I invented *The List of 50.*

I realized that I had never given much *thought* to who I wanted to be in relationship with. I decided that, if I was going to avoid forming another relationship based upon accidental meeting, I had to think carefully about what characteristics I was I was seeking in a partner.

As I reflected upon this idea, I realized that nothing much had changed for me in terms of what I desired as regards *physical* characteristics. I reminded myself that physical characteristics were a poor guide to the depth of a person.

A sidebar: All of this sounds so simple, right? Like - "What an idiot - anybody could figure THAT out!" Yet, when I explain this to clients, everyone, so far, has said, "Wow. I never thought any of this stuff through when *I* formed a relationship."

I started writing a list.

I included the physical stuff, and put it last. Then, I started thinking about how my ideal partner would view the world, vocation, spirituality, communication, relationship building, sensuality, and sexuality, having, (or not having) kids, interaction with friends - in short, everything I could think of that was important for me in a relationship.

I worked at it for a week, adding and deleting as things occurred to me. In the end, I had fifty-two items, which seemed to me unwieldy by two.

I pared the list down to fifty.

I then *studied* the *List* - thought about each item, and refined my language.

- I took out *negatives*. ('I don't want a married man' is not the same as 'I want a man that is single and unattached.')
- I took out vague words - 'I want a good talker' (which could get you someone who never shuts up - I secretly suspect that was what Dar had on her

List, and she got me... as people who know me smile) is not the same as 'I want a person who follows the communication model.'

I went for as many specifics as I could generate. Finally, I had revised the language of the fifty items.

My next task was to put them into order of importance. Having:

1 - blonde haired, and # 50 - follows the communication model

is not the same as having:

1 - follows the communication model and # 50 - blonde haired.

Having completed the task, I posted the *List* (where else?) on my fridge, and read it often.

I then asked myself an important question.

"Do I know anyone who is like this?" Dar immediately came to mind. She'd been a friend since my second year in the Internship, was a teacher of the hearing impaired, and, *from what I knew of her*, surprisingly close in all of the other areas on my *List* (including being blonde with blue eyes...)

So, I called her and invited her out for dinner.

In the early going of our relationship, I told her what I wanted in a relationship and a partner, and encouraged her to think through and decide what she wanted.

The very first deal we made was to spend no less than thirty minutes a day talking about who we are and what we have learned about ourselves that day.

We agreed to take as much time as necessary to resolve any issues we might have with each other, as they occur. I would note that we have not missed a night since starting this in 1984.

We agreed that our relationship would be based upon one, and only one, rule. *That rule is total honesty.* Each day, as we abide by our deal, we speak honestly about who we are and what we did that day. We tell each other everything that we know about ourselves. We listen with curiosity.

As our relationship grew, there were a few rough edges, but surprisingly few, because *neither of us was trying to change the other.* We took the time and energy required to work through the power struggles, and to let them go. My next book, **The. Best. Relationship. Ever.** (due out in February 2013) is all about how to do this, so pick it up!

We have spent our time together learning more about ourselves, while having someone to share that information with.

Anyway, that has been my walk, or a small piece of it. Since 1981, I have been on a pilgrimage into myself. My goal has been to find out who I am today, and to share that information with Dar.

I sit back and listen to what she has to say about who she is. We also take the time to help each other see blind spots. (As in "I notice that you are (whatever) and I'm wondering what your intention is.") This, for us, is the meaning of an elegant relationship.

[ii] http://www.phoenixcentre.com/freebies/watcher.htm

Chapter Five – First Things First

Let's unpack what you are looking for in a mate.

- You will explore significant topics and life positions - things to acknowledge and act upon as you form relationships.
- You will identify what is crucial, what is important, and what is merely icing on the cake.
- In the process, you will likely discover that many of your past relationships, no matter how they seemed at the time, started *because of the icing*.

From this point on, you will base all of your relationships on what is best for your personal development.

Let's get this out of the way first. Behaving in this way is *not* selfish. It is *self-centered*. This is my favourite term, and although some people use self-centered to mean selfish, I use it to mean what it says.

My centre is located in me. I do not want to locate my centre out there somewhere, or to think that my centre is "in" someone else. I do not want to think that something or someone external holds the key to my contentment.

It is crucial that you stop giving away your power to another by pretending that others have the power to make you happy, content, or whole. No one *makes you anything*.

Who I am, how I feel, and how I interpret my life - all of this happens in me, at my centre.

It is not selfish to decide to plan – to work hard – to find someone perfectly suited to share your life.

Find Your Perfect Partner

Imagine that you have decided to backpack in the Rocky Mountains.

Not thinking about the trip (pre-planning,) and taking along a scuba tank and flippers would be inappropriate (and downright stupid.) So, most people who decide to hike in the mountains will do this:

- Read about the topography, wildlife and about hiking in the mountains.
- Read equipment reviews and make a list of things to purchase.
- Head off to a store that specializes in Mountain Equipment.
- Talk to an expert regarding equipment requirements.
- Buy appropriate equipment.
- Pack the equipment so that it can be easily transported.
- Go hiking in rugged terrain, in advance of the trip, to get in shape.
- Finally, after all of that preparation, you head off to the Rockies, and take it slowly and carefully, continually reviewing what you have learned.

What should be patently obvious here is the amount of research, study, and "talking to the experts" that goes into something as simple as backpacking in the Rockies.

The reason there is typically a ton of preparation before any adventure is that the **risk goes down proportionally to the preparation.**

Now, I am not trying to be naïve here. I did not say preparation *eliminates* the risk. That is not possible. What I am saying is that going off half-cocked is likely to mean a rotten hike.

Needless to say, I'm actually talking about your principal relationship. And yet, most people spend more time and effort on vacation planning than learning to find the right person to relate with.

One of the main resistances I get to The List of 50 is,

"Actually thinking about who I want to be in relationship with takes all of the romance out of it!"

What is funny about this line is I have yet to hear it uttered by someone in a successful relationship.

I suspect our reluctance comes from several places:

- Laziness
- Fear of getting what we ask for
- Fear of NOT getting what we ask for
- Believing that thinking about relationships eliminates the romance.

Fear # 1: Laziness is simple. People tend to exert tons of effort toward work, and toward personal projects that they value. But when it comes to relationships, the vast majority of folk think that relationships should just happen.

Fear # 2: Many people think they are better off trusting their lives to the fates. If they ask for something and then get it, it is hard to blame god, society or the other person if something goes awry. .

Fear # 3: This one is even more insidious. People resist asking for stuff because they are afraid that if they ask and someone refuses to give it to them, they are to blame for being unlovable or something. I figure if you do not ask, chances are you will never get what you want.

Fear # 4: Because we in the west are such black and white thinkers, it's common to think that if I focus on *thinking*, I lose the ability to also (and at the same time) focus in on *feelings* and my *heart*. Nothing could be further from the truth.

The heart is *always* involved in relationship issues. What seems to me to be the height of silliness is to try to think with the heart, or to resist thinking at all. Rather than persuade you of this in a paragraph, just remember that *thinking*, while at the same time creating and *fully experiencing* a meaningful relationship, is what this book is all about.

I would encourage you to remind yourself of your experiences with failed relationships, and remember how *blinded by romance* you initially were.

Virtually all of the later disappointments were a direct result of thinking your partner lied to you in the early going - that it was only as time went by that you got to know the "real person."

They did not lie - everything you needed to know was there. *Romance blinds us to what is right in front of us.*

This is why our friends later tell us, "I knew (s)he was a jerk right from the start, but you wouldn't have listened." They knew because they were *not* blinded by romance, and they didn't bother telling us because they knew *we were*!

As your failed relationship progressed, the romance faded.

As it did, you discovered, to your surprise (!!) that many aspects of elegant relating were missing from your relationship. You likely thought that the lack was a defect in *your partner* – a defect your partner wasn't even aware of. Never mind that you were not aware either, until you were...

If you look with open eyes, you will see that failed relationships come from unmet expectations, and the unmet expectations were not noticed at the beginning of the relationship because you were too busy "being in love."

Let me, then, briefly restate, in point form, this non-helpful pattern:

- Boy, (s)he's hot! I think I will go out with him/her. (Lust and hormones = true love.)
- God, this is fun. I hope she/he does not find out what I'm really like. (Honesty is a bad thing.)
- Well, (s)he's certainly different than I suspected. (The dawning of reality.)
- Oh well, I have six months in. I guess I will marry him/her, just in case nothing better comes along. (Laziness and muddy thinking.)
- I wonder how you "do" marriage. I guess I will wing it, toss in what mom and dad did for good measure, and get him/her to change. After all, if (s)he loves me, (s)he'll change to make me happy. ("Love" conquers all, even my partner's dysfunction.)
- I wonder how much this divorce is going to cost. It is better than fighting and being miserable. (The end of another storybook romance.)

I stuck in the parenthetical comments because of my perverse, ironic nature, and after listening to this bilge for decades.

The "system" of relationship failure is simple and predictable and has everything to do with people refusing to think clearly and act responsibly about this very important decision. People spend more time researching which car to buy than they spend analyzing the relationship that they may be in for 50 plus years. How dumb is that?

In the end, all that we can ever hope for is self-knowledge. In a deep, caring, intimate relationship, the relationship is actually a forum for self-exploration. In this kind of relationship, you will dig deeper and deeper into yourself, and then have someone with whom to share the results.

Let's begin this project by establishing your own, personal *List of 50*. I want you to take as much time as you can muster, and really do this job well.

Following will be specific directions, as well as detailed descriptions of the topics you must cover.

Once you have your *List*, we will talk about implementation.

Chapter Six – Who've You Had in the Past?

Initially, *The List of 50* was a counselling tool – an activity that I gave to clients during the course of relationship therapy.

As clients come to talk and work through a dysfunctional relationship, it is essential that they discover what they are doing to *stay stuck* in behaviours that are producing the dysfunction in the relationship.

If the relationship is over, we want to know what they did to break the relationship. In other words, one of the starting places for doing relationship therapy is identifying what *isn't working*, and what the attachment is to *continuing to do* what one knows does not work.

This is not about assigning blame. It is about understanding what you tell yourself about why you do what you do.

For example, as one client described her marriage, it was clear that the sexual attraction the two felt for each other was a driving influence for their getting together. (Her words: "I think we spent the first six months in bed.")

At the beginning, she was also looking for someone to provide her with validation, to tell her what to do, to prop her up. Her husband liked to think of himself as the wisest person on the planet, so he was game – he was convinced he could sort her out.

Over time, over eight years, she found less and less satisfaction from the relationship. She still occasionally attempted to look after him, cook, and clean for him, in exchange for his external validation.

Now, she told me, he just wanted sex, and then to be left alone. He was annoyed that she was beginning to develop a self that was strong and competent, and was no longer completely dependent on his "wisdom."

When she and I started therapy, she was beginning to think about leaving the relationship. She said she was staying because she could not figure out who was to blame for the failure of the relationship.

In reality, she was resisting being the one to make the decision. She was trying to make things bad enough that he'd make the decision for her. She was also staying because she was afraid her parents would not approve of a divorce.

I realized the following about my client's approach to her self and to her relationship:

- She likes to be looked after.
- She likes to have decisions made for her. (That way, she can blame him when things go wrong. When they go right, daddy is looking after her.)
- She has a "thing" about looking young and sexy, and he feeds into this. Yet, after eight years, she thinks (and he says) that he is with her mainly for the sex.
- She needs the men in her life (her husband, her father, her brother... for all I know the Mailman...) to tell her that they are "proud" of her (external validation.)
- She is afraid of being alone, and therefore stays in a relationship she describes as "degrading."
- She is unwilling to be honest about how she has understood and now understands the relationship.

Now, let's imagine, at this point in therapy, (prior to figuring herself and her games out,) that she chooses to end the relationship, (or more likely, makes it bad enough for her husband to end it.)

Without reflection about what went wrong, the next time she decided to get involved with a man, she would simply replicate her past relationship, perhaps with minor variations.

Or, if she chose to do everything differently, she would unreflectively do the opposite of what she had done in the past.

Most people are not this "clever." Most repeat dysfunctional behaviours, learning nothing from the past.

So, in her case, her initial *unreflective stance* would be to look for:

- Someone who likes her 36-year-old body. (After all, she's getting older, and we all know how important "looks" are...)
- Someone who is sexually attracted/attractive. (After all, even though she professes to dislike sex, sex is how you get men to do what you want them to...)
- Someone to tell her what to do. (This time, she'll pick someone who tells her the *right* things to do...)
- Someone to give her lots of positive validation. (Because she *knows* she's worthless, and needs to be propped up...)
- She will definitely change how the new partner looks. (Her present husband is out of shape, which she annoys herself over.)
- She will be willing to barter sex to get the above-mentioned praise and validation. (And then, of course, declare that "all men are alike, only in it

for the sex." At the same time she'll discount the praise she demands of them, because they're only praising her sexual performance.)

During therapy, we brought all of this to light.

She left her husband, and began to consciously and deliberately figure out what she wanted in a partner. She used what she learned in therapy – to let go of her past behaviours – and using *The List of 50*, found a person that was suited to her.

This is why exploring what *did not work last time* is so important. Once you see how you contributed to the failure of each of your past relationships, you'll get a clear sense of what you want, and were not getting.

So, if you were here in my office, I would ask you about your last significant relationship, and also about your other significant adult relationships.

Begin by turning to the Appendix, to Form #1. (Detailed directions are also on the forms.)

Make a list of a few people you have dated, or lived with, or were married to.

- Look for commonalities – what common denominators were there – why did you pick these people over anyone else?
- Pick the most significant, or the most long-lasting one.
- Describe the beginning of the relationship, noting what attracted you, and how the early stages "went."
- Describe the first fight.

- What behaviour(s) did you notice that set your teeth on edge – that you chose either to ignore or to complain about?
- How did *you* handle disagreements?
- Did you attempt to change your partner for the better? How?
- What about your life purpose? Your partner's? (See further explanation, below.)
- What was your sense of yourself during the waning days of the relationship?

Now, repeat the above with a couple or several more relationships, looking for:

- What things attracted you.
- What you were looking for.
- What you got.
- What you were willing to put up with.
- What you tried to get your partner to change.
- Who you wanted your partner to become.
- How you persuaded yourself to stay.
- How you persuaded yourself to end it. (Or, "As usual, he left me," meaning you don't end stuff - people end you.)

An Excursus on Vocation

I use the word 'vocation' interchangeably with several others, including life purpose or calling. I will repeatedly ask you to explore the vocation of your partners, as well as your own. This means I assume that we all have a vocation.

Here is a definition:

A vocation is a "directional pull" toward a way of being in the world that is, at once, inward and outward directed. It is outward directed in the sense that to be vocational is to be in or of service to others. Yet the vocation is profoundly inward, as the point of the vocation is the strengthening of one's self knowledge.

A vocation causes you to focus in and narrow down your attention, as opposed to being scattered all over the place.

Many personal struggles are nothing more than people trying to be all things to all people. As an illustration, a client told me: "I give 110 percent to work, and 110 percent to my ball team, and 110 percent to my charitable work. I don't have much left, maybe 80 percent to give at home."

I pointed out to him that his lack of math skills might have something to do with his exhaustion, and then asked him why he thought he needed to give so much.

He replied, "So that people will tell me I'm doing a good job and that I'm a good person." Thus, his life purpose is: "To work my butt into the ground, to the detriment of my family, so that others will make me feel good about myself."

He just might want to think about that one.

Another illustration: A client tells me she has learned a lot since her divorce. She is now an advocate for empowering other separated and divorced women. She sees herself as their teacher.

When questioned on how that plays out, she says that she preaches at them, and they all want to be like her ("I'm up on a pedestal!") She spends most of her time, either on the phone or in person, solving their problems, which never seem to stay solved.

Her life purpose actually is: "To talk a good show, be admired and be endlessly needed by a long list of helpless women, while never having a life or actually living what I'm preaching." Given her *real* life purpose, she will continually be in relationship with needy people who will expect her to solve their problems, and blame her when their lives come unglued.

In my own case, I once described myself vocationally as a joyful agent of change. What I meant by that is that I provide the guidance and environment for others to make the changes they choose.

As regards my ex-wife, however, I got things twisted around. I was not very joyous, and I was trying to make her change into who I wanted her to be, for her own good.

My vocation, with her, was something like; "I am the wise and all-knowing therapist / husband who is going to save her from herself." (One of my therapist friends once yanked my arms out as if I were hanging on a cross, and said, "We've already had one (a Messiah) and it didn't work out for him either, so you can stop auditioning for the job.")

Anyway, work through the first form, and also give some thought to the vocation question – who are you, and why are you here?

Chapter Seven – The Contents of a List of 50

So, what is supposed to be on the List?

Well, what did you discover as you explored past relationships?

- Some aspects of the relationship worked perfectly, and they belong on your *List*.
- Other aspects were missing – you realized this, over time. Just remember what you really desired – those things you tried to turn your partner into, and failed.

If you look at the work you did in exploring your past, you should see many things that you made into continual sources of irritation and anger. Start there.

These are the items that become the basis for your *List of 50*. Each is stated in positive language (more on this later.) Things that "didn't happen" in your past relationship(s) are reframed into statements of what you *do* want.

In my past marriage, a "negative" was: "Is not interested in what I do for a living if it interferes with her schedule or priorities." This would be reframed: "Is interested and excited about my vocation," and "Is comfortable rearranging her schedule when unforeseen events arise."

Here are a few from my List, so you get the idea. Don't copy!

"Interested in (enquires about) me – in the person I am today."

"Expresses her curiosity, and openly states differences of opinion."

"She tells me who she is today, and every day, using the communication model." (I know what "the communication model" means to me, as I teach it and use it all the time, so therefore I do not have to spell it out.)

"Vocationally, is in a teaching/helping profession. She continually develops her skill-set, and provides excellent information without attachment to whether her student/client 'gets it.'"

"Light hair, preferably blue eyes."

These issues, or rather their opposite, were the "deal breakers" that led to my divorce.

To repeat, in my relationship with Sue, we were continually at odds over (among other things) which of us was "right" about how to communicate. And, we were on opposite sides of "make a living / living a vocation."

There was no give and take, no curiosity, on either of our parts, as both of us were heavily invested in being "right." As for work / vocation, there was endless debate and disagreement, again with no hope of resolution.

The reason there was no hope is simple.

Some things, like what to have for supper, or where to go on a holiday, are issues or topics we are only slightly or moderately invested in.

When it comes to *crucial issues* (say, the top 5 or 10 on *The List*,) the issues are not really issues. They are descriptions of my *self* - of the core of my being. They make up the core of me – who I am and how I function.

Core items are not debatable.

My sense of vocation, for example, is as *intrinsic* to my personality and "self" as my blue eyes, and as Sue's approach to work was to her. Because of this, a challenge to the way I "live my working" is not the same as a challenge about the clothes I choose to wear.

My "living my working" *is* me. My clothes are *about* me.

I saw vocational challenges as attacks to the core of me. Sue saw it the same way - I did not agree with her choices, so she thought I was attacking **her**.

Our core principles run deep. Because they "are" us as opposed to "about" us, attacking core issues and turning them into a debate about "right and wrong" *always* leads to anger and resentment.

Added to this is that what is "core" for me might not be "core" for you. You may not value honesty and good communication. That doesn't make you "wrong." That makes you someone I ought not to be in principal relationship with.

Why? When it comes to the principal relationship, being with someone who differs on a fundamental, core level (again, say the top ten on the *List of 50*) can do nothing other than create tension, anger, resentment, and endless fights.

I would therefore say emphatically that disagreement in the top 5 or top 10 means that the relationship is completely unworkable. *With the top 10, there* **must** *be consensus – period.* Beyond that upper level, there is more flexibility.

A sidebar: on "Right, Wrong, Opinions and Facts"

One of the things we have to understand if we are going to be healthy, and have a vital relationship, is the *relativity* and *subjectivity* of how we see the world.

We desperately want to believe that the way we see things is "objectively true" (in other words, verifiable or common knowledge, like gravity: "a force which keeps us from flying off the face of the earth.")

Not so! *Nothing* we believe about our internal selves, and *nothing* we believe about who others are, is empirically "true."

The "way I see it, is the way I see it," and nothing more.

I usually qualify this by saying that what is "true" is what I perceive. Dar's eyes, empirically, are blue. As are mine. The words I hear her say are the words she said.

However, and this is what I am getting at, what she meant by her use of those words, and what I assume she meant, is not "true" or identical. Our interpretations – our stories – get in the way.

I have a client with a bad back. I've been working on it, using Bodywork, for years. During that time, she has said, "I'm a westerner. What am I doing wrong mechanically?"

I talk a little about that, but have also been suggesting that her emotional state and energy flow are "behind" her weak back. Today, she said, "I think I'm beginning to see what you mean. My belly (seat of passion) is blocked."

Now, it's not that I was "right all along." And, no, she doesn't completely agree with me. It's that I listen to her, and she listens to me, and our beliefs are flexible. They flow together. And, as she was discussing her pelvis, her hips and pelvis were "wiggling," for me a sure sign that her body was agreeing.

In a sense, our lives are nothing more than the stories we tell ourselves.

Absolutely nothing in our lives is understood by us, or even received by us, objectively (by this I mean devoid of any meaning that *I put on it*.) We filter everything in our lives through our previous experience. If a situation is "new," it is filtered through what we determine to be the nearest comparable situation.

A personal or relationship crisis often happens when the story we are telling ourselves is too narrow to contain the "crisis" experience. We're back to "tension." Psychologists and existentialists call this "anxiety." It's the gut sense of discomfort (a sense of doom, perhaps) that happens with core conflict.

There is nothing more "true" than this: What you see is what you decide you want to see.

Let me give you an illustration. "Mary" became a widow two years ago, at age 35. "Objectively," she is just that - a widow. The story she tells herself (her subjective experience,) however, is not that simple.

On one level, she still "feels" married. On another level, she is "the grieving widow." Thirdly, she is a single woman looking to "get laid" and get on with her life. This is also her order for the three identities.

Mary, as "the widow," wants a man to hold her and comfort her. She finds this tricky to set up, as her "hold me" request is often interpreted as a prelude for sex. She meets her need to be held through barter. "You hold me; I'll return the favour with sex."

Having sex is OK with "the single woman," but the single woman has an additional agenda - to turn the sexual intimacy into a relationship leading to marriage. Otherwise, the sex would be "wrong."

To add to the confusion, "the married woman" thinks that, when "the single woman" has sex, she is cheating on her dead husband.

"Objectively," this seems simple. "The Widow Mary" wants to be held. It is, after all, verifiable that Mary is, indeed, a widow. The "problem" arises when the single woman and the married woman show up on the widow's date.

Mary is actually trying to achieve something for which her self-definition has no room. This is not about her *actions* - it is her *interpretations* (the story she tells herself) that mess her up.

It should be clear that the story of Mary's life is neither consistent nor broad enough.

Now, let me hasten to add that the goal of therapy (and life!) is *not* to find the true, "objective" story. There is no true, "objective" reality. All there is, is the story you are telling yourself.

And here's the point: if your life seems stuck, you must change your story. As you change your story, you change your filters

Far from there being *limited* choices in life, the limitations we find ourselves confronting are artificial and unreal constructs, created in advance by the stories we tell ourselves. As the expression goes, "Argue for your limitations and they are yours."

We have the potential, in dialogue, to examine and re-examine the stories of our life. We can listen to what we tell ourselves, how we describe our situation, and we can begin to understand that, far from seeing our lives objectively, we see them quite subjectively, and find ourselves living self-fulfilling prophecies that are limiting and limited in the extreme.

Until we change our story, and understand that our stories are just that. Not true - just stories.

Crucial Themes

There are themes that are "large ones," and for most people are quite significant. I'd like to suggest that you begin by exploring these key themes, and work toward understanding two things:

- first, what the themes mean for you, and
- second, how you would like your partner to "be" regarding the theme. As I wrote above, one way to do this is to review what you were looking for, and not getting, in past relationships.

I want to note here that I am not, in any of the illustrations below, setting up a right / wrong, good / bad dichotomy.

These Crucial Points are the issues that clients bring to therapy - differences in one or more of these areas are what leads to divorce!

There is no judgement here about what's better or best. What is important is this: As far as these Crucial Themes go, in general, agreement is essential!

These Crucial themes are not in any particular order.

Vocation:

As I have described it above, vocation is my language for the person's raison d'être; their life purpose, or reason for being. Given your own understanding of how you function in the world, how do you see the person you are seeking "being" in the world? What will drive him or her - motivate him or her? What is his or her "passion?"

I want to be clear here, so let me spell out a common way vocation becomes a problem.

I will set it up using a familiar 50s stereotype that still exists today. Dad decides to be a successful executive. His goal is to rise high and make money. Mom wants a close-knit family that spends a lot of time together.

Now, clearly, much of the tension would go away if the man and woman focused *either* on career and money *or* on quality family time. There is going to be a problem when one person wants one, and the other wants the other.

Now, where this really goes off the rails is when the couple refuses to see that they have a *vocational* difference, and instead fight about "whether Fred is being a good dad."

Fred thinks, "Boy! Look at all the money I am bringing in. Our quality of life (the stuff we have) is much higher than when I was growing up. My wife and kids have every advantage. Am I ever a good dad!"

Wilma thinks, "What a lousy dad Fred is! He is never home, the kids barely know him, and all he wants from me is the occasional roll in the hay. When is he going to realize we want him, not his money?"

Good dad? Bad dad? Irrelevant, as both positions are "right" - from each individual's perspective. The question not being addressed is: what is the vocational force driving Fred? Wilma? Are they *compatible*?

See how important this one answer is?

Life Focus:

This issue is crucial. What is the person's order of priorities? In a sense, we just addressed it in the Fred & Wilma example, as vocation leads to a certain ordering of priorities – which takes precedence.

Here are a few examples:

Fred: work, making money / investments, clubs, and friendships that can help him with the first two, kids, "down-time," Wilma, relationship.

Wilma: kids, relationship, house, family directed activities, Fred.

Remember my client who was math-challenged and kept thinking he could give 110 percent to several things?

His order of priorities would be: work, team, charities, family, and wife.

Mine would be: Self-knowledge, relating with Darbella, vocation, intimate friends, family.

This is the time for brutal honesty. Do not be politically correct here. Be brave and actually put things down in the order that is true for you.

You might have noticed that my *priority list* was the only one of the 4 to include "me." *Please* remember to include *you* on the top of your priority *List*. Sadly, most people will either leave themselves off, or put themselves close to or dead last.

Spirituality:

Some of you may have found my Messiah reference, about having my arms stretched out, to be funny, others might have been taken aback, and some might have found it annoying or offensive.

Religion and spirituality, or even the lack of same, is typically a buzzy topic. You therefore want to be crystal-clear in your definition of what you want in this area. Differences here can become extremely significant. My sense is that you and your partner ought to mesh here. Even if the meshing is, "spirituality is not important to me." (see also: *sexual preferences*, below)

Political views:

Have you noticed that I am listing the things that "mommy" told us not to discuss at parties? –wink- Remember: you are looking for someone to live with *forever*. How will it go if you fight for job creation and equality and your partner thinks welfare recipients are lazy? Get my point?

Spirituality and political views are also about *ethics*. Our politics and our spirituality are often used to *explain* and *justify* the way we treat others, our family, and ourselves.

- If I consider others to be irredeemably damned to hell because they engage in certain behaviours, I am going to be reasonably rigid in my approach to ethical issues.
- Or, I might think that ethical decision making often happens in the gray area between black and white.

- Or, if I have a squishy, new-age, wishy-washy approach, where nothing is bad or wrong, but rather is simply a misunderstanding, I will be impossible to pin down in a relationship, as I will be unwilling to think I have to decide anything.

The spiritual person in relationship with the non-spiritual person may spend their days trying to "enlighten," convert, or "save" the less spiritual person. This is where "I'm only doing it for his own good" comes into play. And it's a nasty play, indeed!

Communication style:

Of course, I am prejudiced in the direction of the model I teach. My model, the model Darbella and I live - involves total honesty, with full disclosure, and elegant and deep communication.

Bennet Wong and Jock McKeen teach an excellent communication model, which is explained in their book, *The NEW Manual for Life*. (Wong, Bennet & McKeen, Jock, 9-15) If you'd like to read their model, the text of the six pages concerning the communication model can be downloaded from

www.phoenixcentre.com/freebies/special_page.htm

You really need to decide how you will communicate with your partner, know the *details* of the model you choose, practice it with a therapist or a friend, and INSIST upon this model as a prerequisite for building a relationship.

Left to our own devices, most of us communicate incredibly poorly, and get sucked into dramas at the drop of a hat. Thinking that you can forego the preparation in this area, and either wing it or sort it out "if" there is ever a problem is short-sighted, which is another way of saying, "dumb."

Do whatever it takes; spend whatever it takes, to learn to communicate well.

Sexual preferences:

I have worked with many couples whose sexual style, need for closeness, touch, foreplay, and eroticism simply do not match. Both thought the other would "get over it." Wrong. Think about what you need. Settle for nothing less.

Virtually all sexual issues begin as communication issues, whether it's not quite getting what you want and hoping someday it will happen by accident, to refusing to discuss and come to a consensus on frequency, to disagreeing on what behaviours are ok with you and which ones are not.

So, extend your communication style into the sexual arena, as in, "S/he will use the communication model to talk through sexual differences."

Be specific! Fundamental difference is sexual preferences can be a deal-breaker!

One list I recently saw demonstrated this. One item was: "is a conservative Christian, and practices his faith." Another item: "Is into polyamory, group sex, and bondage."

No, really.

Now, I know another couple who have been together for years, and these two items *are* on their *Lists* – extremely kinky sex lives, and fairly fundamentalist Baptist. They've made it work (obviously they don't talk about their proclivities at Church...) – but this is quite unique, in my experience.

Just keep in mind that, in general, sexual preferences and spirituality are often entwined!

Sexual "Fidelity":

It is the height of silliness to think that just because I am in relationship with someone, I will stop noticing everyone else on the planet.

Being sexually attracted to "non-partners" is scary for most folk, and discouraged in the west. Yet it happens to all of us, all the time. We encourage (naturally) honesty regarding how one feels about and toward others.

In other words, one of our goals is to desensitize people regarding being sexual, so that sex and sexuality become normal as opposed to special.

At the very least, you and your partner have to be on the same page around extra-relationship sexual feelings and actions. Again, do not be politically correct and leap to writing "sexually monogamous" if that is not what you know you want.

And recognize that this is one area that likely will change over time for either or both of you, so (as I wrote above) you want a *List* item, "Is comfortable with sexual dialogue."

Physical appearance:

You know... no point ignoring this area. I am listing it here to get you think about what really rings your chimes.

I'd like to persuade you to drop physical appearance from the Top 10.

On the other hand, blonde and blue-eyed seems to be important to me!

This is the time to discover what your "physical flash points" are. (If you are not sure, go sit in a crowded Mall for an hour or two, and let yourself "feel" the pull of physical attraction, and narrow things down for yourself.)

Spare time focus, activities:

Clearly, all of us have a list of things that are important to us – our "non-vocational passions." These might include hobbies, physical activities, causes, and other interests.

You want your partner to also be interested in them, and perhaps, depending on their importance to you, passionate about them.

Often, in *dysfunctional* relationships, the partners will judge their partner's passions to be silly, or immature, or a waste of time. Ever heard something you care about described that way? Ever describe a partner's activities that way?

By way of an illustration, a friend of ours was over one day, and she and I were having coffee and a cuddle and discussing "life." She is quite into painting, and is taking courses. I was asking her how it was going, and she said that she really had not painted anything in a while – that she didn't have time.

I asked her what making time would look like. She said, "I'd get all of my stuff in one place, set up a canvas and say, 'I'm painting for the next 8 hours. Everybody, f**k off!'"

I smiled and said that I was actually turned on just hearing the passion in her voice.

Now, imagine what would happen if her partner thought painting was "cute," or "silly," or "a waste of time." Trouble, in spades.

Intellect:

In general, I believe that your *IQ* should match or approximate your partner's. Partners do not have to have the same field of expertise.

The key is an intellectually *level* playing field. This allows you to elegantly resolve discussions WITHOUT one party dominating the other because of intellect.

It is not that "smart" is better than "less smart." It's that having a significantly different IQ means an automatic *imbalance*, and a pull for the more intelligent person to become the teacher of the less intelligent person.

Emotional Intelligence:

This is a semi-new concept, brought to the fore in a book by the same name. (Goleman, Daniel) The idea is that, in addition to "mental intelligence" (IQ), there is Emotional Intelligence (EQ). Goleman suggests that EQ is both a measurable and "trainable" intelligence.

I think that the average EQ, in terms of age, is about 16. In my counselling practice, my client base is middle class and up. Virtually all of the people in my practice are reasonably to highly intelligent (IQ) people. Yet, their relationships are crumbling because of EQ stupidity.

One client told me:

"I get home from work and as I walk up to the door, I think how much I missed my wife. I am so looking forward to seeing her. Then, I think how much I want a hug and kiss. When my hand touches the doorknob, I think that it will be so nice to see her run up to me and hug me. Then I go inside, and there she sits, refusing to move, wanting me to *go hug her*! So I just go upstairs and pout."

Guess what? Their relationship is not working.

Once he saw why, he began to take responsibility for fixing his side of things. His EQ has jumped by a decade.

There should be parity of EQ. I do not want to be in a relationship with someone who is going to pull out all stops to attempt to manipulate me through emotional battery. I want to be in relationship with someone who has her full range of emotions available to her, and who is willing to own them.

Example: High EQ: "I am making myself sad right now, and I need to cry. Would you be willing to sit with me while I cry?" Low EQ: "See! You have made me cry again. You're a terrible person!"

Short hand: One major measure of high EQ is the willingness to accept responsibility for what you are feeling, own it, and get over yourself. Low EQ people blame their partner.

Place on the Introversion / Extroversion scale:

There needs to be harmony here. I have met people who are far apart on this scale, and who have a successful relationship. Mostly, though, I see that introvert / extrovert couples seem to spend a lot of time apart, after the initial dating stage of trying out the others' style.

Two extroverts will likely spend a lot of time with many other people, but will do this together. Introverts will be pleased to curl up at home, together, for conversation and reading.

Midlines will have a balance of being alone and spending time with others. Wide divergence in this area is likely an obstacle to deepening intimacy.

Sidebar: You are not seeking a Clone

I am going to need to emphasize repeatedly that the goal of *The List of 50* is *not* to find your clone.

Darbella and I are quite close in how we choose to be with each other, and sometimes miles apart on issues. We sometimes have, for example, heated discussions about the quality of education in Ontario. We do not agree about the quality of education, as compared to, say 20 years ago.

However, underlying this is our *total agreement* regarding the importance of vocation. I do not question (nor attack) Dar's dedication to teaching. Thus, the question is about the quality of education, not about whether being a teacher is a good thing.

Scott Peck once said that one reason to be in relationship was for the friction, which I took to mean the *tension* created when two people with fundamentally unique operating systems have a dialogue.

That being said, I choose, in my significant relationship, to be in dialogue with someone who has at least visited the planet I live on, and has some appreciation for my worldview. A clone? No. A co-walker along the path? Yes, indeed.

Getting Started

Use the ideas above, (and other areas of importance to you,) as a jumping off place for finding *50 characteristics* you wish for in a partner. For now, just write ideas in point or sentence form, as they pop into your head, and as you reflect on past relationships. (Feel free to browse the Appendix for samples of what others have written, but don't just copy! This is about you and what you want and need.)

Think about Friendships with Same Sex Friends

I was describing the *List of 50* last week, to a client. Her marriage had recently ended, and she was contemplating the future. She said that she was at a loss to understand her relationships with males, and was worried about the future.

In the same breath, she mentioned the excellent relationship she has with her best, female friend.

I said that she might want to look at what makes that relationship so special and functional.

She replied that it had to do with their ability to speak honestly with each other, using a direct form of communication. They accept the other as who they are, and are willing to listen without trying to force the other person to change.

Hmm. Does that sound familiar?

My point to her (and you) is that she *already knows* how to form an excellent, working friendship that is deep and intimate. She knows how it works and what makes it special.

It is illogical in the extreme to think such a way of being will only work with her woman friend. The *specifics* are unique to that relationship, but the broad strokes of their friendship are repeatable ad finitum, with men as well as with other women.

She found a friend with whom she meshed. She needs to notice and apply the same rigorous standards in her next relationship with her next *partner*.

Chapter Eight – Down to the Basics

You've got your 50, right??

Before we talk about the next part of the project, let me tell you a story.

Some years ago, I was working (separately) with two female roommates. They had both had relationship breakdowns, and were exploring the why's and how's in therapy.

As it turned out, I mentioned *The List of 50* to them the same week. They liked the idea, talked about it at home, and decided to go to Toronto for the weekend, get a hotel room, drink some wine, and compose their *Lists*.

They had a great time, enjoyed the differences in their *Lists*, and decided they were ready to meet a partner that fit. They expressed amazement at how different their *List* was from the men they had dated in the past, and seemed to "get" how easy it is to get off-track when you do not have a map.

Within six weeks, both had met someone who closely matched their *List*. Very closely. Both were thrilled. The entire counselling session with each of them was spent exploring techniques for deepening their relationships while practicing good, intimate communication.

However, a few days after that week's sessions, they called me and were angry. They said, "This *List* thing of yours doesn't work. It's a disaster!" They booked an appointment to come in, together, to confront me. I agreed.

In they walked. They were quite agitated. I pressed for what had happened. After much descriptive language, one blurted, "Both of the jerks are married!" I smiled, and asked, "So, did either of you have "Single" on your *List*?"

Silence. Then, one said, "Damn!" and they got up and left, to revise their *Lists*.

After revising their *Lists*, in the next six weeks, both had met a single man who fit. I like both of the men. They suit the personalities of the women. The women jell with the men.

So, is "single" on your *List*? Is the sex of the person you are looking for on your *List*? Is the age bracket of the person on your *List*? How about sexual orientation? One client recently missed this step. She now has a new, gay, best friend!

While you may have thought of all of these, it is important to be clear. In order for you to find who you are looking for, being specific is a necessity.

Thinking, for a minute, about business

I am a practical person. As a therapist, I am constantly looking for analogies and stories that will help clients to "get" what I am saying. The reason I use analogies and stories is that many people tend to get insulted if I am too direct.

Since most of my clients are in therapy for personal issues, finding a parallel non-personal illustration is quite helpful.

I've noticed that most people seem to ask intelligent questions and make concrete plans when their businesses are concerned. So, I often use comparable business analogies – situations similar to the issues the client faces - situations in which the client is experiencing success.

So, here's a good analogy: at work, we draw up business plans, speak to advisors, hire accountants and advertising consultants, and constantly monitor our cash flow.

Imagine our business lives if we thought that things should happen by *chance*!

- I want to encourage you to take your relationships as seriously as you take your business.
- I want you to invest more time and energy into your relationship than anything in your life except for your personal self-development.
- I want you to be ruthless about rooting out behaviours you engage in that do not work.
- Please, accept the idea that being specific about whom you are, what you want, and how you want to live out your life in relationship with others is a vital task!

Review your *List* on this basis: the principal relationship you engage in is the arena in which you have the best chance of truly finding *yourself*.

So, go polish your *List of 50*.

Sidebar: on Non-Attachment

One of the tenets of Zen Buddhism (and of Buddhism in general) is the idea of Non-attachment. This concept is often connected to things, as in "letting go of attachment to money, or position, or one's house."

Perhaps the most overlooked Non-attachment is letting go of attaching to beliefs, concepts, and principles.

What I am suggesting is the necessity of letting go of your past views of relationships.

Because of our attachment to keeping our beliefs intact, many do not learn from their mistakes - they are not willing to accept responsibility, and then change, how they relate.

What is essential is to let go of thinking that excellent relationships happen by chance, or because you have met your "soul mate." Rather than blaming the cosmos for relationship failures in your past, accept responsibility for them. Not blame, responsibility. It might sound like this.

"I accept that I expected the right person to simply fall into my lap. I now know that I put little or no effort into deciding who to be in relationship with, and my lack of effort is one major reason for my failed relationship."

Here is the non-attachment part:

"I now know that defending the romantic notion of relationships is silly in the extreme. I will let go of this notion, and fully accept my responsibility to choose my relationships carefully. I will do this, not because there is no romance in the world, but because depending on romance to the exclusion of conscious thought and clear action simply does not work."

Non-attachment, then, is the conscious skill of thinking:

"Does this thought or action deepen my self-understanding and achieve the results I seek, or does it create what I profess to be resisting?"

Letting go of a cherished belief can be a daunting task. Nonetheless, letting go is required here.

Chapter Nine – Examining Your Language

Self-responsible language is a first step in figuring yourself out.

This is a way of communicating designed to encourage you to speak *truthfully*. It is also a way of speaking that expresses clearly your ownership of what you are feeling, thinking, judging and doing.

As a simple example, rather than saying "You make me so angry," you say, "I'm really angering myself." Similarly, you define who you are in the moment, and what you want, as opposed to reeling off an endless list of what you *do not* want.

I would strongly suggest that the vast majority of "couple issues" are, at their root, language and communication issues. Examining your language is an essential skill, and we begin it here.

Your *List of 50* must be *accurate* and *clear*. Ambiguous language leads to bad results.

Back to your list.

Negatives

As I mentioned in the introductory remarks, you must remove negatives from the list. Negatives leave too much room for interpretation. What I mean is that a negative tells me nothing about what the person *does* want. I am still left guessing, and the person issuing the negative is "off the hook."

As an illustration, a client said, "I don't want my daughter to turn out like me."

I said, "So, knowing your life experience as you've described it to me, that would mean you don't want her to be a single parent at 38, with no job, no relationship, and no hope?"

She agreed that this was exactly what she meant.

I said, "So, I guess it would be OK if she was a 15-year-old prostitute and heroin addict?"

She looked horrified. "No, that wouldn't be OK!"

"Well," I replied, "she wouldn't be like you..." She nodded and smiled. I said, "Maybe, instead of saying what you don't want, you'd like to say what you wish for your daughter."

As regards your list, then, my point (which is obvious) is this:

"Not married" is not the same as single. It could get you someone who is engaged, dating, or separated. I suppose it could also get you a priest...

"Not a heavy drinker" could get you a woman who gets loaded on two glasses of wine, or a man who is rabidly anti-drinking.

"Not into sports" could get you a person who weighs 400 pounds, eats cheezies all day, and watches soap operas.

Go back over your list. Look for any place where you used a negative. Find another way to write any negative items you find.

For example, change "Doesn't hurt me" to "Is emotionally, spiritually, and physically caring and is positively demonstrative."

Be specific about what you DO want, not what you do not want!

Ambiguity

Look also for ambiguous language.

- "Likes to talk" is different from "Follows the communication model," or "Elegantly balances speaking and listening."
- "Into the outdoors" got one of my clients a gardener who never left his property. She was looking for a hiker.

I might write, "Is actively involved in Zen living, humanistic personal growth, and deepening her core beliefs."

For me, *actively involved* means "is doing work on herself, not just reading about it."

If you choose to take a shortcut (like "is actively involved") and you know what you mean by the shortcut, that's OK. The goal, as always, is being clear with yourself.

This is a vital point. One of the causes of relationship difficulties is ambiguity, or being attached to thinking that everyone "knows" what a word means.

Ambiguous example: "Wants to go out to dinner regularly."

Now, what does "regularly" mean?" Clearly, in a room full of people, the number of dinners out that equals "regularly" will vary.

Also, "Wants to go out..." is ambiguous. "Goes out..." is not.

Such vague words are the genesis of endless miscommunications.

Finding the Words

One of the "arts" involved in the *List of 50* is finding the words. Sloppy thinking and language contributes to most of the things we do not want showing up in our lives.

If you have not seen the original version of the movie "Bedazzled," with Dudley Moore and Peter Cooke, rent it.

The plot: a short-order cook (Dudley) sells his soul to the devil (Peter) to win the love of the waitress at the restaurant he works at. He gets 7 wishes.

No matter what he wishes for, because of his imprecise language, he gets what he *does not* want. The devil, obviously, is in the details. (There is also a scene about worship, involving a fire hydrant, which is worth the price of the rental.)

The reason we laugh at this movie is that it rings so true.

In order to create an elegant *List of 50*, you have to be aware of the meanings you attribute to words, as well as how vague words can be misconstrued.

Back to your List. Pretend that your list is a project for publication. Your goal, with each point, is to capture the essence of what you want to say, in positive language, in as few words as necessary to convey your meaning carefully. If your list ends up being three pages long, who cares?

Chapter Ten – Ordering the Cosmos

Now is the time to read your *List* and establish priorities. Despite the fact that all 50 items are important to you, and you have spent a lot of time honing them, now you need to work at ordering the items by their overall significance.

It is good to be perfectly honest and admit that we do not tend to think about the *importance* of particular characteristics when thinking about our primary partner. Because of the myth that it is all supposed to *work out*, somehow, by magic, the farthest we get is a good-bad list.

This kind of thinking makes everything of equal importance. Living our lives this way is a sure path to disaster.

For example, for me, communication is paramount. I also like order and neatness. Dar would agree about the importance of excellent communication, and would be much less into the "order and neatness" thing.

Now, imagine what my life would be like if I made "good communication" and "is neat and orderly" of equal importance. I hope you see how stupid this would be, but in case you do not, let me spell it out.

If I make orderliness "important," then each out of place coffee cup will be elevated from a misplaced coffee cup to a 'comment' about Dar's 'feelings' about me. In other words, I would be elevating a coffee cup to the point of taking it personally.

You may think this odd, but in therapy the problems addressed are often of the "coffee cup" variety. I think this is so because people do not have the remotest clue about prioritizing.

Once we begin to see that some things we want in a relationship are add-ons, some are useful, some are important, and some are crucial, we will begin to understand how issues that came up in past relationships escalated into major battles.

We want to remember that the exercise we are engaged in here is intensely personal. My goal in life is to figure myself out. I have mentioned it before, and repeat, I believe that "my order of relationships" unpacks this way:

1) My goal in life is to observe and understand what I can about myself, every day.

2) I am in relationship with Dar - she has "volunteered" to act as my principal witness, an interested listener - who hears me as I talk about what I know about myself, each and every day.

3) She is in the process of endlessly "unpacking herself" and chooses to share herself with me. We have agreed to be present with each other, listening and interacting carefully and clearly. We are open and honest with each other, having no secrets from each other.

4) Beyond each other, we each have a small group of "intimate friends" with whom we can choose to share ourselves.

So, I work on me first and foremost, and then share what I know of me with Dar, using our communication model – working from a place of "compassionate relationship."

Therefore (as he finally comes to his point...) the "highest priority items" on my List might read:

1) My ideal partner is actively involved in self-exploration, and is using or is willing to use a humanistic psychotherapy model to do so.

2) Is committed to total honesty as the basis for the relationship.

3) Discusses herself and our relationship, in all of our dialogues, using the communication model.

4) Is actively involved in deepening her spirituality through use of Zen principles and activities.

5) Will devote no less than 30 minutes per day to intensive conversation with me, as above.

6) Is open, honest, and vulnerable about herself, and will be present with me so that I can be the same with her.

Now, this short list is just for illustration purposes, and other items may actually be on my *List*.

I am setting this up, though, to show that the above #1 *is my number one item*. For me, this is essential. Therefore, it HAS to occupy position # 1.

Head to your *List*. Develop a scheme for prioritizing what you have written down. The top of the *List*, obviously, will contain the most important items. Shift the items around and when it feels "done," write or type the list neatly on good paper.

Chapter Eleven – Be a Poster Poster

You might want to make copies of your *List*. For sure, you want to put your *List* where you will see it. I put mine on the fridge, as I said, and carried a copy in my DayTimer.

Your commitment is to read over your List often, no less than three times per day. For at least 25 days. The theory behind this is that it takes 25 days to get rid of a bad habit.

As we said when we were discussing filters, filters are predispositions, or habits - ways we choose to "see things." There is nothing particularly valid or "true" about any of them.

Nonetheless, they operate subconsciously and pretty much perfectly, and the only way to "change a setting" is to repeatedly bring what we want to change into consciousness. This leads to the creation of new neural pathways (new "habits," if you will.)

The more often you can "reset your List" by reading it through, the better.

In order for the new way of seeing to become real for you, you need to *study* your *List*. In a sense you're moving from a place where the *List* is a theoretical construct to where it becomes your new reality.

I'd almost suggest that you overdose on your *List*. You can't read through it too often. Repeatedly tell yourself, "This is the kind of person I want to be in relationship with." Practice, practice, practice!

Spend time each day visualizing interactions with the kind of person you've described in your list.

- Think about creating a meaningful and deep conversation with this person. Imagine depth and intimacy as you engage in direct and truthful discussion.
- Imagine spending time with this person. Visualize day-to-day interactions. Hear yourself elegantly working through day-to-day decisions, and quickly resolving obstacles.
- What will it be like to engage in mutually satisfying activities? What's the sex going to be like? How will you fight? What will it be like to resolve each issue as it comes up, rather than leaving it or stuffing it?

The goal is to make your new way of interacting with this person "real." If we do not imagine the new behaviour or perspective as being available to us ("real") the likelihood is that it will not become real.

Remember, the person you are describing actually does exist! That is an absolute given. Your job is to know what you are looking for and to visualize meeting and interacting with this person. Take this seriously!

I mentioned that, as I looked at my *List*, Dar popped into my head. I didn't know her really well, but did know her as a friend. She seemed to fit the profile I'd made for myself.

It seemed a small thing to call her up and ask her out.

From square one, I was honest with her. I told her I had thought about her and realized she was someone I wanted to get to know as a potential life partner. I said I was intrigued about what I did know about her and wanted to learn more about her.

I invited her to spend some time thinking about what she wanted, while she got to know me in this new context.

The discussion continued (it's still happening) as we revealed who we were, and what we wanted – as we learned to communicate with each other.

In a sense, we were "comparing our Lists" to see how well they matched.

As the relationship deepened, we each felt more comfortable letting go of our need to hide from each other, and entered into the process of open and honest revealing, both of ourselves and of our wants and needs with each other.

Think about the people you know – allow your intuitive self to compare your List with your "available" friends and acquaintances.

Because people in our lives are filed away in categories, we disregard whole groups of people because they are not in the "dating material" slot. Your task is to ask yourself, "Is it possible that I already know someone who might fit my *List*, and that I simply might not have thought about that person in this way before?"

No sense reinventing the wheel if the person is already in your personal orbit.

Chapter Twelve – The Big Question

I have intentionally left something out of the game we're playing.

I wanted you to engage with me in what has actually, right up to this point, been a theoretical, head-game sort of exercise. I wanted you to draw up the *List* after an exploration of how you have "done" relationships in the past vs. what you really want in a relationship now.

You needed to do this cleanly and without any kind of pressure or fear. The *List*, in other words, *needs to exist on its own* - as a tool and a perspective about what you want from your relationships.

The List, up until now, has been a task unto itself.

Having said that, it is time to push on and really challenge yourself. The question you need to answer is,

"*Am I ready to begin a relationship with the person on my List **right now**?*"

Often, in conversation with clients, I propose the *List* exercise and the immediate reaction is, "I'm not ready for a relationship!" I encourage them, as I have encouraged you, to do the project anyway. The reason is simple.

I am convinced that the reason relationships fail is a *serious lack of paying attention*.

The List of 50 exercise, to this point, has been to get you to really think about your relationship history, to explore what has worked and what has not, and to commit to focusing in on what you want and how you are going to get it.

The mere existence of your List almost guarantees that things are going to begin to shift, whether you want them to or not.

As we go back to the idea of filters, it is clear that resetting filters means that we "see differently." You have been working on the *List* for a while now, and I suspect you have begun to notice, as you drill the points of the *List* into your subconscious mind (through repetitive reading and visualizing,) what kinds of people you are starting to meet.

I can virtually guarantee you have begun to meet people of both sexes who fit your description. Friends, co-workers, matches are beginning to pop out of the woodwork.

Finding a person to spend the rest of your life with, however, will not happen *until you are ready.*

If you are not prepared to begin a meaningful relationship, the person might show up, and one or both of you will be aware that the timing seems off.

You are programming your subconscious mind to seek, to filter in (help you to notice) *only* people who fit your *List*, and your subconscious mind will do precisely, exactly, and only that.

Filters are functioning all the time, and function, for the most part, out of our consciousness.

I do not have to decide which sounds to filter out while I am typing this, for example. I want that process to be automatic.

Moreover, to again "prove" the obvious, I can be typing and suddenly realize that Dar is talking to me. I say,

"Suddenly realize" because my filters are set in "typing" mode, and I do not consciously hear her.

Then another sub-filter, for "Dar's voice," seems to kick in. It identifies the "blocked sound" as her voice, and "suddenly" I am aware of it.

Now think about it. Her voice did not "suddenly" start. An unconscious shifting of filters "suddenly" shifted it from my unconscious to the conscious level.

The point is, filters are real, and filters can be changed, or re-set. We do it all the time. We are just not aware that we do.

The reading and repeating of your *List*, over time, has imbedded it into your sub-conscious, *over the top* of your previous filters. This imbedding is why you are noticing so many "appropriate" people coming into your life.

However, until you also give yourself permission to filter in or factor in the "I am ready to build a deep and intimate relationship" idea, you will simply end up with many interesting friends.

So, are you ready? If you are, add a line to your list, at the bottom, something like:

"I am now ready to meet the person I've described and begin to develop a deep and lasting relationship with him/her."

A caveat: I just mentioned that your new filters are being written "over the top" of your old, dysfunctional ones. Maybe it's better to say they're written "alongside." I say this to warn you of a common issue.

You will walk into a room and your old pattern will kick in, and you will spot the kind of person you have always been attracted to, even though, in the past, the relationship has not worked out. You will need to **consciously trigger your new *List*** and remind yourself to focus on it.

Chapter Thirteen – The Friend Factor

As I've just written, the *List* is not only a description of whom we choose to be with as our primary partner.

It is also a List of characteristics describing who our best friends might be.

Most adults have no clue why they have the friends they do, and some actively dislike their friends. But they seem to think they are "stuck with them." This happens because we often make friends on auto-pilot.

Many adult friendships are based on *proximity.*

For instance, two of my college roommates were "proximity friends." I got to know them and ended up being friends with them because they lived in my room, so to speak. The first was someone I really clicked and related with. Even after he switched to another University, then moved to the west coast, we kept in contact by phone, visit, and letter.

My next College roommate and I had little in common beyond a slight over-indulgence in recreational substances prevalent at University in the early 70s. He had a great sense of humour, and I even included him in my wedding party for my wedding to "Sue." In 1975, Sue and I moved to Canada, and I have not heard of or from him since.

Another way we "end up" with friends is through *social activities.*

They invite you over, you invite them over, and soon you end up spending time with them, but the conversation may seem quite limited, as the real basis for spending time together is the activity.

Best friends are people *chosen* because of a deeper connection.

These are people I have *chosen* to be with on an altogether different level than acquaintances. I have a fair number of acquaintances, and a short list of best friends.

Here is my point: My best friends match my List closely. This is not a coincidence.

What I am getting at here is that you do not have to be friends with everyone who wants to be friends with you. You do not have to be friends with people who only want you to endlessly listen to their tales of woe. You do not have to be friends with people that, after they leave, cause you to roll your eyes and say, "That was terrible."

If you drain your energy around someone, a friendship with that person will simply be - draining.

Use your *List* to evaluate each of your relationships. How many of your friends match your *List*? Surprised by your answer?

You may want to look at changing some not-so-great friendships to acquaintances.

Then use the *List* to attract a circle of people who are on a path similar to yours.

I am amazed at how many of my *clients* match my *List*; people who are at the point of wanting to explore how to find their vocation, are confused about meaning – are looking for guidance as they dig deep and find themselves. This is the power of doing your work – creating your List.

Chapter Fourteen – Why This Works

The List of 50 is not magic. There are legitimate reasons why it works.

The first explanation will be of a Spiritual nature, the other scientific.

A Spiritual Approach to Manifestation

This is a time-honoured way of looking at our relationship to the cosmos, which is also described as "the abundant universe theory." Jesus once reportedly said, "Ask, and you will receive."

Other religious traditions also say that we get what we focus upon. In Chinese medicine we learn, "Energy flows where the mind goes." (A simple biofeedback exercise taught to migraine sufferers is to raise the temperature of their hands a degree or two. This is quite easy to learn. Moreover, it demonstrates that we can program our minds, using "new" tools, to make changes in the "real" world.)

The opposite of this is, "Focus on nothing, and you will get it."

All of this unpacks to the idea that we live in a neutral universe. You might look at "the cosmos" or "life" as a classroom, designed to provide the lessons we need, or lessons designed to remind us of what we already know.

Life, much like school, is like this: if we do not figure out the lesson, we get to repeat it and repeat it until we do get it.

(Some people never get past this point - sort of like being stuck in detention forever.)

Where we can get bogged down is having the expectation that once we learn a lesson, the issue is "over." Nothing could be further from the truth.

Much like real school, we learn lessons so that, the next day, we can tackle harder problems. (The same issue, made more difficult.)

Thus, in school, learning to add leads, not to "no more math," but to subtraction, to multiplication, which leads to algebra. And on and on.

This applies to *The List of 50* in many ways. For example, the *List* causes us to examine who we are bringing into our life through *inattention and desperation*. If we never get beyond "God, I'm so lonely. I need a (wo)man," we can't blame the cosmos for the weird people who show up for the "cast call."

It is like going to Wal-Mart with no shopping list. Amazing how many "daily specials" hop into the cart. They almost seem to have a mind of their own.

On the other hand, go into the same store with a shopping list, focus on the list, and you have the possibility of going home with the items, and *only the items*, on the list. (Well, at least you will have a better chance than with "no list.")

There is a simple functionality to all of this, and it has to do with the cosmos working toward getting us to be more specific. Another way to put this is that the cosmos is asking us to pay attention - to be "in the moment." Many people go through their lives on autopilot, recklessly careening from one near disaster to another. Paying attention is a simple cure.

To pay attention means to notice, without judgement, what is working and what is not. It is about refusing to cling to, or to attach to what is not working, simply because we invented it.

True spirituality, it seems to me, is a quite practical thing - it is all about doing a lot more of what works, and very little of what doesn't.

The List helps us to think deeply about the characteristics of the people we want in our lives, to visualize such people, and in this way to "draw" them into our lives.

This is actually an erroneous way of describing the process, but seems to fit for many people. What is actually going on, as we have been describing throughout the book, is that we are re-setting our mental filters to exclude those who will not be useful partners, and filtering in those who will.

Thus, my preferred description is the scientific one.

A Scientific Approach to Filtering

I've written about filters several times in this book, and it bears repeating - filters are the result of our beliefs - I consciously or subconsciously head in a certain direction, and in that process, create filters that dictate what I see, hear, etc.

The subconscious mind does this task quite willingly. It is actually an essential skill - otherwise, we would be bombarded with sights, sounds, smells - and would be so distracted as to lose our ability to focus.

Where this wonderful system goes awry is when we set a filter without knowing we have set it. Alternatively, we set a filter because we are afraid.

Prejudice exists because of such unconscious settings.

If we assume that "All Martians are evil," our subconscious mind will, without objection, filter out 99 good actions by Martians, and make large the one evil act reported in error on the nightly news. And we say, "See! I told you! All Martians are evil!" (You may, of course, substitute the prejudice of your choice.)

As to meeting someone, as we have said above, many people do this non-consciously.

A woman, for example, may love her father. She absorbs *her interpretation* of his characteristics, and they become the characteristics she "looks for" in a partner, without even knowing she is doing it. Voila. She only notices, "Men like her father." Then she wonders why the men she ends up involved with treat her like a child.

On the other hand, perhaps her father met her every wish and desire. She now has subconscious programming that contains the expectation that males will treat her like a princess. It is a long stretch from "My daddy treats me like a princess!" when one is six, to "I am a princess, and men should take care of me, because I'm really, really special!" coming from a forty-year-old.

Even seemingly benign filters can come back to bite you.

I was in grad school with a woman whose first husband was a psychiatrist. Their marriage lasted eight *weeks*; they were into a power struggle from the get go. She had what I would describe as a "princess filter," expecting special treatment, and the psychiatrist did not think she was very special.

In other words, he dared to disagree with her.

She spent a lot of time talking to me about men, and how they had to behave. She would start with, "I want a man just like you," and I would laugh at her because in the next breath she would be angry with me for not taking her seriously.

Rather than think through her past failures, she decided to "mount" a campaign to find Mr. Right.

She took a summer job as a Camp Director, and decided she was going to "land" one of the male staff. I would get a letter each week, describing this week's Mr. Right. All the stories would come out about why the "flavour of the week" was *perfect*.

Then, something would go wrong, and she would be on to the next guy. She got to the last week, and only the custodian was left.

Her last letter before the end of summer arrived, along with a request that I pick her up. She wrote, "I want a man who will listen to me, respect me, and treat me like a queen."

The custodian fit the bill. All he ever said was "Yes, dear. No dear. Whatever you think, dear." I just about retched when I met him. Lester Milquewheattoast. After a year, she married him.

She showed up on my doorstep four years later. The marriage was over, she said. Why? "All he ever does is agree with me. He has no opinion of his own. It's like I'm talking to myself."

Sounded good on paper, though, eh? Not.

We had a long talk about how she had set herself up, and how she needed to figure out what she *really* wanted. She shook her head at my ignorance, and let me know, gently, that it was a *fluke* that she kept meeting "loser men."

Ah, well…

The List of 50 is food for the subconscious. The subconscious is designed for and LOVES projects like this one. Of course, what you are doing (through re-reading the *List*) is *programming* a new set of filters.

This is also why you can keep the *List* posted after you meet your partner, change the sex to "male or female" and find a whole group of interesting *friends*. Or you could rewrite the list to specifically target clients, mentors, or therapists, whatever.

Once the filters are in place, your subconscious will not let you easily "see" people who *do not* fit the profile. It will thus appear that the only people you are meeting (other than, say, clients, who you "have to" meet) are people who fit the *List*.

From a "Spiritual" perspective, it is like the cosmos is providing what you need. From a subconscious, scientific perspective, what is happening "makes sense."

It is not magic. Manifesting the things we need, the lessons we need, has a sound basis in both our spirits and our minds.

Chapter Fifteen – Some Closing Thoughts

The List of 50 is a technique, and like any technique, it takes time and effort to learn and implement.

Once you complete this project, you will see many applications for this technique, in your career, with your children, as a "healthy lifestyle" practice - the healthy lifestyle one is actually a good one - we "get over" ourselves by re-imaging what is happening in our bodies. (This is the whole point of visualization techniques in cancer therapy.)

Left to our own devices, we can be incredibly lazy about what, if anything, we focus on. We tend to get lousy results, and blame the situation, our parents, our genetics, the Progressive Conservatives, whatever.

The List of 50 brings us back to ourselves, and requires of us due diligence. It is, after all, our life we are talking about.

The discipline involved in living a focused life is dramatic. Our culture is anything but disciplined, and the sorry state of the world is a direct result of sloppy thinking, over-generalization, blaming, scapegoating - all ways to avoid the rigorous discipline required to master your life.

The List of 50 is one simple technique for adjusting your focus, clearing your mind, and stating who you are and whom you want in your life.

If you would like to learn more about living a disciplined, whole life, help is at hand.

I have bundled together three of my best books, *This Endless Moment, Living Life in Growing Orbits,* and *Half*

Asleep in the Buddha Hall. They are each about finding yourself, changing the patterns that do not work, setting out in new, vocational driven directions, freeing yourself from the blocks that have kept you stuck.

You can read all about them at:

http://www.phoenixcentrepress.com

Lastly, we love hearing from you! Please also let us know how you liked this book AND of course let us know of your experiences with the *List of 50*.

Lovingly, Wayne

waynecallen@gmail.com

The Forms

Form #1, page 1 – Who've You Done?

Hint: DON'T write in the book!!! Use a notebook!!!

- Begin by creating a list of adult relationships you have had. This list should include people you have dated seriously, and anyone you have been engaged to, or married.
- Now, pick the most significant relationship. Write the name down.
- Describe, in detail, what attracted you to this person, from first eye contact through the first few dates. How did (s)he treat you? Is there a standard description for the relationship? (i.e. prince/princess, parent/child, teacher/student, confessor/penitent, sex object, wise, all-knowing person/seeker after "the truth.")
- As the relationship progressed, what was the first fight about? How soon did it happen?
- What behaviour(s) did you notice that set your teeth on edge, but you chose either to ignore or to complain about?
- When you disagreed about something, what did you do? What did (s)he do? Did you work each issue through, or just fight about them and leave them unresolved?
- Did it ever occur to you (or did you make it your purpose) to change your partner (for his/her own good, of course!) into a "better" person? If so, (and I am talking to everyone now, right?) what did you want in the "changed person?"
- What about the other person's life purpose? I use this word interchangeably with vocation or calling.

- What was your sense of yourself during the waning days of the relationship? In other words, what were you willing to put up with?

Go back to your list of people, and, using another copy of Form # 1, do the questions again, regarding another person. Do several, then come back here.

Now, use the rest of the notebook page to summarize what you have learned about how you "do" relationships, and how you are "done." Imagine that you are at a WRA (Weird Relationships Anonymous) Meeting and it is your turn. You are going to tell the assembled masses what you are recovering from.

In 1983, mine might have gone: Hi. I'm Wayne ("Hi, Wayne!") and I'm recovering weird relationships junkie. I've been attracted to blonde, blue-eyed women since I was a teen. I saw it as my mission to figure out what they were doing wrong in their lives and set them straight. I wanted a woman who would be my equal emotionally, mentally, spiritually and vocationally. So I did the logical thing. I hooked up with women who were completely different from me emotionally, mentally, spiritually and vocationally and attempted to persuade them to change. Because I saw them as projects, I never seemed to be done, content, and happy. Now, I've hit bottom, and have decided to give up on changing people so that I can be happy.

Now, write yours.

Form # 2, Scratch Pad for The List of 50

Using the guidance the book provides, start to jot down *on a new sheet* a list of characteristics you want in your principal partner. Please remember that the language must be positive ("I want") not negative ("I don't want.")

Form # 3, The List of 50

On top of a blank page, write:

This List of 50 belongs to _____

Using the ideas you created above, write your List of 50, and then use the suggestions in the book to polish it and put it in order.

Comments about The List of 50

How wonderful to hear from you, even if it is a group mailing ;) I'm pleasing myself over the fact that you are writing a book on the List of 50. I find it ironic actually because the timing is rather impeccable. I finally, after 6 long months of emotional and physical celibacy decided to re-write my list. This time I did a good job, not a half assed job as I was so used to doing in the past. I really used the tools in the booklet; I examined my old patterns, past relationships and myself and came up with my true List of 50. At the time I re-wrote it I was going through something with an old friend as soon as I severed the negative relationship I allowed myself to find the man that fit my list 100 percent. I actually showed him the list and he laughed and said "You wrote this after you met me didn't you?" I hadn't, as a matter of fact I had written it about 4 weeks earlier. XXXXX and I have spent the summer together getting to know one another and each other's children and we are enjoying all that goes along with it. I have also been using tools from building long and lasting relationships and I am finding that they are truly helping me to not go back to old patterns. I am honest with him and with myself and I rarely give anyone other than myself the power to make me feel anyway. I find this one different in the sense that I have built my own security and I no longer feel a need for urgency. I am not rushing things and still enjoy time on my own. Whenever I see myself slipping into my old patterns I simply stand back and observe without judgment and correct where I am with self-awareness and of course breath.

Find Your Perfect Partner

Having downloaded four of your booklets, it is my pleasure to offer you the feedback you are requesting. I have read through the three on relationship and find them to provide useful information in a clear, well documented manner. I am planning to teach a course entitled "Understanding Human Relationships: Counselling Skills for Educators" next term and will suggest my students check out your website and, perhaps, download the booklets themselves.

I have attached my List of 50. You are welcome to use any or all of it. (I borrowed a few of your suggestions and modified them). I might be ok with you using my name if I knew the precise context in which it was being used. I have used affirmations and intentioning before and know the power we each have to create our realities. I also agree that the more specific we are the better. When I showed my list of 50 to one friend he commented, "Do you have a short list that us mere mortals could aspire to?" My answer was, "I had a short list and it got me my ex-husband. I'm being more particular now."

Does anyone fit my list? Well, I have "tried" a relationship with one man that almost fits my list but a few of the very important points were not met (high energy, engaging fully in life being the most important). Having the list made it very clear. He remains a very, very close friend so that's a good thing. I have "reunited" with a fellow I went out with some 32 years ago who has potential for fitting my list. I say potential because it will take time to know. We live in different provinces, which is a difficulty, of course, but seem to be beginning to explore the possibility of relationship over the phone for now. (By the way, I've suggested he read the booklet and write out his own list. I'm kind of hoping he'll notice I fit his. Might not work that way but I'm willing to take a chance.) This latter connection, made after I had written my list, has me think that it really is possible that someone out there could fit it. so that alone has been beneficial.

A final thought. As I re-read my list (not quite daily but frequently) it is clear to me that besides the qualities that are specific to another - height, profession, etc.) the qualities I want in a man are the qualities I work towards for myself. That is, being a person of integrity, caring, committed to my psychological and physical health and development. It was interesting to note that. Not surprising, just interesting.

I worked on THE LIST OF 50 a while back. In the end I don't think I ever had exactly 50 items but it was close. The first real date after doing the list -- (remember the "chargy bit"..xxxxxxx...that doesn't count though:)) came the following January...it was xxx (remember him?...) and that lasted for about 3 months...fun to start but I soon realized that I needed to renew my list (I wish I would have kept the original). I updated it with some pretty practical things like... "My partner doesn't smoke" and "My partner doesn't snore." In the end, he dumped me (a good thing for me to experience) as he really didn't want (or wasn't ready) for relationship...or the kind of relationship I thought I wanted.

I re-wrote/refined it again in May and early June... I met xxxxxxx on June 16th. I had to laugh when I read it again and saw the one about wanting someone in the greater Toronto area. I've lived in Burlington and that did not work for me...interesting (and oh so extreme...:)) that I should find xxxxxxx right in my back yard! For the most part I think I got much of what I was looking for...in the ideal sense and in some pretty practical things too (no smoking, no snoring, no allergies!!). Overall - I'd say I got at least 85 percent of what I wanted... so far!

Find Your Perfect Partner

I wondered how much "the order" mattered after I did it the second time and so I did move some things up on the list. Although, the "wanting my partner to enjoy and share in the cooking" was close to the end, I have to tell you (she says almost embarrassed) that I haven't cooked a meal for over a year!! I really got the full meal deal on that one! And interestingly, my attention to the physical appearance and age did not manifest. xxxxxxx missed the top end of the age limit by about 6 years! More significantly I attracted someone who really does want to be in relationship, is eager to learn and grow and explore new ways of living and being (i.e. making different choices.)

I did "copy" some of your ideas and desires for a partner, which I think you will know when you see them. After all, and to this day, I tell xxxxxxx...that if it wasn't for my experiences with you and Dar I would not have been at the level of readiness I was, when we met. I also took some advice from the "Conversations with God" book around the power of prayer and changed some of it to present tense language (i.e. My partner is ...vs....My partner will be). I believe that helped speed-up the universe's response! You know me and language...I still hold true that much of my growth has come from looking at and changing my language. I've been reading "Language Structure and Change" again and it all seems to make more sense now. Xxxxxxx has really shifted his language since we met and has seen how it has changed his relationships.

I think the most significant "getting what I wanted" was my number one point - which I think was yours... "Above all I am in relationship to learn more about myself." I am getting just that. As we enter into more and more of the power struggle, as I learn to get over myself time and time again.. I see just how lucky I am to be on this journey. Of course, when we "found" each other...on the surface, we were attracted by our similarities. I find more, as we go deeper, that it is our differences where I am really learning about relationship and about self/other compassion.

I am now using the List of 50 in a general way to re-focus my career and my relationship with money. I have never had a good relationship with money and...it's time to get out of my own way around that...and to quote you...oh dear, sweet you...it's time to step up to the buffet of life and choose a hell of a lot more than chick peas!

The List of 50 is great stuff. I read it immediately after download, and made a list immediately after reading. But I gave myself a lot of pain/sorrow/struggle/internal turmoil after making the list realizing the husband I have is not or the opposite of the first few qualities I wanted. It is also an eye-opener. I realize how come I was so unhappy.

It triggers a lot of emotions, when the clarity is there, there is no longer room for lying and not knowing. But still it is a lot of risk to leave the known and go for the unknown.

I did not look for and meet any guys 'cos I was legally married and morally unavailable.

But it certainly helps me to recognize what I missed from the marriage, and eventually it is easier to let go and agreed to make the decision for the divorce, 'cos it will give me the chance to really look for the guy for me later on when I have finished my recovery.

I'll be glad to give feedback on your "The List of 50". I found it to be very useful in the healing process from my divorce. I have recommended it to several people who were in relationship transition stages. Many have used it. Those that have have found it helpful.

I'm currently in a relationship (about 9 months) that has been built around the concepts and learnings from my list. In fact, I recommended The List of 50 to this woman, who revised a list she built earlier from different criteria.

Our lists, and the concepts in them, have been an active part of our dialogue in our relationship.

My list has been an active part of my relationship building since I drafted it. I have modified the list several times, based on how relationships worked out. It was also interesting to note, how few elements of my list my ex-wife matched, similar to what you said about your first marriage.

I feel that using the process you recommend does improve the quality of the choices you make. Of course, building the other relating skills will complement this as well.

These are my thoughts in regards to the List of 50.

Most of all, it made me consider things that I'd never really taken the time to think about. Previously, I didn't know that I had any say or any control in who I ended up with. It brought some reality and control into that mysterious, magical world of Love.

It was a challenge to think of the 50 qualities I wanted in a partner. I think I maxed out around #38. I was forced to evaluate my previous relationship. I thought about what worked and what didn't.

That said, I did realize that if I choose to get involved with someone who is lacking any of the characteristics that I have on my list, I would be well aware of it and wouldn't be surprised by that fact 6 months down the road.

Overall, I think this exercise gave me control in my personal life by offering me choices, and leaving me with the responsibilities of my decisions.

Yes, I read "The List of 50" as soon as you had published it, and spent several days carefully compiling my list based on what I hoped I had learned about myself from previously failed relationships.

Boy, and how it did make sense! Yes, the list is included. I implemented the list to some degree. I met a man shortly thereafter that proved to be too good to be true. I discovered I had ignored the 'honesty' feature / factor on the list (# 37). Believe me, it is the one thing I have paid more attention to since. I was overwhelmed at the insight the "List" had provided! And I still am.

Now, I have recently found someone who meets nearly every item on the list. By 'nearly' I mean that some things that weren't 100 percent, we are working on together. Discussing them until we reach an element of understanding between us, about what I want or expect, or what he wants and expects. I think this is called negotiating. His current concern is that he will be 'using' me (# 44) if he allows me to give of myself to him.

Example: I am an RN, and he needs to have a hernia repaired soon. Due to other physical problems (COPD and related heart problems) I offered to stay with him for a few days until he has recuperated. He has a doctor's appointment to set up the surgery this coming Monday. He has agreed for me to go with him to that appointment! And I'm sure the rest will follow.

Find Your Perfect Partner

Each of us has had problems with low self-esteem..... Maybe this is about to end. I also think it might be appropriate to show him my "List" and even share my copy of the booklet with him. His wife died almost 3 years ago and he feels he is still dealing with that loss. He is still depressed (on medication), but not to the extent he was when we first met 5 months ago. He is having problems with some sexual dysfunction, but that seems to be on the mend as well. I am learning to be more patient.

I want to give you an update on the effects of my List of 50. I very much was wanting a relationship in the spring and summer and, after writing out my list, read it often and gave it to a number of friends, both as a "giving it away" and as a request for fixing up. I was also aware that I really did need time alone to get deeper into my own Being, to learn to feel not just comfortable but happy with being alone. This fall, although there was still a part of me wanting relationship, I clearly accepted and decided I more wanted to be alone, for the present at any rate. My life is full and I have plans to be away next year on sabbatical. A conscious relationship takes time and effort and I was happy to work on my self alone.

Well, as we know, giving something away seems to be the major ingredient in receiving. Three weeks ago I met the cousin of my friend and within 3 conversations we both knew this was for life. Timing was excellent as we both had holidays and spent a week together. The knowing only increased. He matches 49 out of my list of 50! (And I already have a good car mechanic so I can easily give that up.) Loving has never been so easy, so sacred, so healing. Thank you.

Other People's Lists

List of 50

1. He loves me for who I am today.

2. He accepts my child as my child.

3. He prioritizes; Himself and loved ones, career, family and friends.

4. He is male, single and unattached.

5. He accepts my need to grow intellectually, emotionally and spiritually.

6. He has a sense of humour similar to my own.

7. He is loyal and faithful.

8. He is trustworthy and honest.

9. He enjoys sex with me frequently.

10. He is between 29 and 33 years old.

11. He is between 5'10" and 6'3" in height.

12. He is between 180 lbs and 230 lbs

13. He is physically attractive to me.

14. He is physically attracted to me.

15. He enjoys traveling for pleasure.

16. He enjoys his job and is good at it.

17. He is creative.

18. He lives within 30kms of me.

19. He is affectionate with me.

20. He communicates his needs, desires and emotions to me.

21. He listens when I speak.

22. He opens his heart to my needs, desires and emotions.

23. He holds my hand.

24. He hugs me with his whole body.

25. He calls me to see how I am doing.

26. He has spiritual beliefs similar to my own.

27. He is romantic and tells me he loves me.

28. He believes in commitment and monogamy.

29. He enjoys spending time alone with me.

30. He enjoys the outdoors.

31. He enjoys going out socially.

32. He is outgoing.

33. He enjoys walking, swimming and being active.

34. He is easygoing.

35. He is intelligent.

36. He loves animals and children.

37. He respects my need to spend time alone.

38. He looks into my eyes when he speaks to me.

39. He has a good relationship with his family.

40. He has lived alone.

41. He is responsible for his own emotions.

42. He saves some money for retirement.

43. He is generous with his time in regards to me.

44. He enjoys the same kind of music I do.

45. He has a healthy body.

46. He loves who he is.

47. He is kind caring and trusting.

48. He is aware and acknowledges his behavior.

49. He responds rather than reacts.

50. He accepts my family.

Another *List of 50*

1. He is single, emotionally ready and wanting a committed relationship.

2. He loves and is able to be loved.

3. He is in good psychological health and committed to his psychological understanding and spiritual growth; he processes his thoughts and behaviours, reads and attends workshops and follows a disciplined practice in order to enhance his development.

4. He welcomes intimacy, enjoys processing and will give the time required to "work on" the relationship.

5. Closeness and physical affection are important to him.

6. He has a high, but not hyper, level of energy and engages in life fully.

7. He is intellectually, emotionally, spiritually and vocationally my equal and treats me as such.

8. He communicates mindfully with open honesty and inquiry.

9. He has enough money to satisfy all his wants and needs now and in the future.

10. He is able to express the full range of emotions and is willing to own them without dumping on or blaming another.

11. He gets excited learning about and enjoys discussing new ideas, concepts and possibilities.

12. He is in good physical health and committed to his physical well-being; he exercises regularly (preferably including Taoist tai chi), follows good nutrition (little red meat or sugar), and balances work with play.

13. He is a man of integrity, compassion and a strong sense of morality without needing to impose his standards on anyone else.

14. His order of life priorities are personal development, relationship, family, vocation, friends, community.

15. He finds fulfillment and enjoyment in his work without it taking over his life.

16. He works from his heart as well as his mind.

17. He is comfortable in his sexuality, enjoying both giving and receiving pleasure.

18. He is a sensitive lover, interested in exploration.

19. He will be interested in and accepting of me as the person I am today, without the need to change me.

20. He will be supportive of my interests and personal life journey.

21. He will be present for my process, allowing me to express my vulnerability.

22. He is open and honest with himself and others.

23. He has a good knowledge of human psychology and enjoys discussing and learning more in this area.

24. He has a gentle nature with a strong presence.

25. He is even-tempered and easy going, finding joy in living. He is generally happy and loves to laugh and be playful.

26. He is generally an extrovert who enjoys socializing with others although he also enjoys quiet time alone.

27. He enjoys being physically active in outdoor activities such as hiking, canoeing, and cross-country skiing. He is less interested in being a sport spectator.

28. He loves to travel and to have different experiences and has sufficient money to allow us to travel comfortably and engage in activities that we choose.

29. He enjoys dancing, watching and discussing movies, and listening to a variety of music, particularly opera, classical and folk.

30. He enjoys foreplay and eroticism without making sex of primary importance within the relationship.

31. He is between 52 and 60 years old.

32. He is between 5 ft. 6 inches and 5 ft. 10 inches tall.

33. He has a solid body with a strong chest and arms. His weight is appropriate for his size.

34. He is a kind and generous person who feels comfortable to show his caring nature to and for others.

35. He will be able to hear my experience of him without becoming defensive, even if it is not what he wants it to be.

36. He will share his experience of me in a manner that is considerate and sensitive.

37. He is able to speak with authority without being arrogant.

38. He welcomes the opinions of others, especially when they are different from his own.

39. He is a socialist although he may not be actively political.

40. He is grounded in and likes himself and is able to laugh at himself.

41. He has an artistic outlet and gives time to its pursuit.

42. He tokes or drinks only infrequently and does not smoke tobacco.

43. Vocationally, he is in a teaching/healing profession.

44. He lives close enough to Brandon that we can easily spend time together as frequently as we choose.

45. In his view of life, the glass is always half full.

46. He can work with his hands, do household and car repairs, and problem solve.

47. He is clean-shaven.

48. He has his own home and wishes to remain in it for now.

49. He will enjoy and be enjoyed by my family and friends.

50. He will love me deeply, honestly, unconditionally.

Another... *List of 50 –*

1. Above all I am in relationship to learn more about myself.

2. I am in relationship with someone who wants to know and be with me and is open to me knowing and being with him. I am in a relationship with someone who wants "relationship".

3. I am in a relationship that has open communication... honesty, respectful and intimate. I am engaged in true dialogue (thinking and feeling together) with my partner and we are in the on-going process "in-to-me-see"... revealing ourselves to each other...

4. My partner is open to loving and accepting my son as he is - and he is a significant part of my life. He openly accepts my son's father as a part of my life. He will spend time with my son with me and not be resentful.

5. My partner is open and accepting of my brother and his life partner.

6. My partner engages in "I" language communication and authentically integrates the belief of "self-responsibility".

7. I am in relationship with someone who is interested in taking good care of himself (body, mind & spirit) and his health.

8. I am in a relationship with someone who takes the entire "package of me" and explores with me the concept of "unconditional love".

9. My partner makes as much money or more money than I do and is interested in making money as a source to freedom, having experiences and adventures.

10. My partner has a sense of humour and takes himself "just short of seriously".

11. My partner does not snore.

12. My partner does not smoke.

13. My partner is willing to experience the fullness of all experiences (good or bad). We play and seek adventure in our relationship - exploring the richness and of life.

14. My partner has an attitude of appreciation and gratefulness for the richness of living in the moment.

15. My partner can be with me in my quest/pursuit of understanding and learning about my own life process. I rarely say "good enough" when it comes to this.

16. I share this life path with someone who inquires more than he advocates...he is inquisitive/curious and he listens to understand...without judgment and the need to be right.

17. I am in a passionate and romantic relationship. My partner is open to exploring the intimacy of shared sensuality, sexuality, charge and passion.

18. My partner talks as well as he listens (in bed and out).

19. My partner actively engages in his own personal growth and quest for deeper meaning. He has done some kind of "self-awareness" work and he continues on his journey.

20. My partner will is interested in people. And he is open-hearted to others and is vulnerable in his process.

21. I am in relationship with someone who understands and participates in my need to grow and explore myself, my connection with others and spirit.

22. My partner is balanced...knowing when to apply all aspects of his personality in any given situation.

23. I am in relationship with someone who is patient...so, I may understand and attempt to integrate patience into my life.

24. I am in relationship with someone who is curious about transpersonal approaches to life (body, mind and spirit).

25. My partner is interested in his "vocation" and how he can grow in exploring that process.

26. He is single, male, between the ages of 38 -50 and is emotionally available.

27. My partner is interested in travel.

28. My partner spends and enjoy time with my family. Specifically, he loves to participate in the care of my family cottage on the East Coast.

29. My partner enjoys cooking and sharing in the process.

30. My partner is not be allergic to cats, dogs, or dust.

31. My partner is connected to nature and enjoy exploring the beauty she provides.

32. My partner is open to my "scheduled" approach to life but will also enjoy spontaneity when possible.

33. My partner lives/work in the greater Toronto area.

34. My partner will be willing to consider re-locating at some point to B.C. and/or Nova Scotia

35. My partner enjoys music and dancing.

36. My partner is maximum 5ft 9" tall. Blue/Green eyes and blonde or light brown hair.

Another *List of 50*

1. seeks to understand (accept) and learn about people and the world, is curious, asks sincerely, listens to the answer

2. is truthful and sincere, in the moment, regardless of audience

3. displays range in feeling, emotion and expression, takes responsibility for them, extreme to extreme and points between

4. is balanced in investment of time/resources - being active and inactive, between work & play, etc

5. is direct in communicating her needs and wants

6. is fit as a result of an active/healthful lifestyle and diet

7. is independent personally and politically, thinks for herself, and expresses those thoughts

8. over 42, less than 51 YOA

9. intelligent, from both education and experience

10. is flexible when dealing with differences

11. can say she was wrong and I'm sorry, when appropriate

12. has friends and activities, some separate, some where I will be included

13. pretty face and figure

14. Likes/wants physical intimacy, hand holding to sex, initiates occasionally to often (twice weekly/twice monthly)

15. slim to just into HWP

16. takes interpersonal risks

17. has chosen success as a goal, where competition was a factor, achieved it, and acknowledged it

18. has led and/or is a leader

19. divorced or experienced in loss, learned from it, and is now available for relationship

20. is spiritual in a holistic, organic way (includes Eastern thought)

21. is creative in problem solving

22. is aware of what's happening in the world

23. kids are OK, prefer childless

24. appreciates and interacts with nature, such as gardening, pets

"List of 50":

1. Someone who loves me as I am.

2. A man whom I can love as he is.

3. A man who will just listen, and resist trying to 'fix' things, unless asked.

4. A man who has his own likes/dislikes and will share that sometimes.

5. Someone who will share my likes and dislikes sometimes, too.

6. A man who is financially secure.

7. Someone who has a terrific sense of humor.

8. A man who is generous with himself, his time, talents, money, etc.

9. A man who is compassionate.

10. A man who is sexually attractive.

11. A man who is sexually attracted to me.

12. Someone who is spiritually based and can support this.

13. A man who is willing and able to communicate in order to resolve issues.

14. A man who loves me. He may at times dislike my behavior, but loves me anyway.

15. A man who wants to please me, surprise me, and spoil me, etc.

16. A man who knows who he is, what he wants, what his priorities are, what he will tolerate in other people in general.

17. A man who has no secrets because he has shared all of them with me on a deep level.

18. A man who is passionate sexually.

19. A man who is physically attractive and takes care of himself.

20. A man who is clean, a nice dresser, and impeccably groomed.

21. A man with comparable intellect, but different areas of expertise.

22. A man who is willing to be wrong and doesn't have to be "right".

23. A man who is physically, emotionally, spiritually caring and positively demonstrative.

24. A man who can discuss/deal with his emotions and mine as well... will just hold me while I cry, for example.

25. Someone who can discuss issues without attacking me, either verbally or physically.

26. A man who enjoys being at home alone together, reading, cooking, cuddling, just doing nothing....

27. A man who enjoys fine dining, theater, concerts, etc. often.

28. A man who enjoys long walks together.

29. A man who has a limited, if any, desire to use alcohol.

30. A man who is a non-smoker.

31. A man with controlled eating habits.

32. A man who enjoys pampering me, and enjoys being pampered

33. A man who can speak without offending.

34. A man who can listen without defending.

35. A man with consistent moods, i.e., usually upbeat, happy, pleasant, etc., and is tolerant/understanding of my moods when they aren't always the best.

36. A man who is able to verbalize fear, sadness, instead of resorting to calling it anger.

37. A man who is totally open, up-front, and honest.

38. A man who is single, available emotionally and spiritually, and willing to consider a committed relationship with me alone.

39. Someone who is male, age 68 to 72, heterosexual.

40. A man who enjoys limited sporting events, with or without me.

41. A man who can 'be present' with each other, interacting carefully and clearly.

42. A man who is willing to be vulnerable with, and with whom I can be vulnerable.

43. A man who is a true helpmate.

44. Someone who is a giver and knows how to accept being given to.

45. A man who is polite.

46. A man who is sensitive and caring.

47. A man with whom I can develop a better level of self esteem.

48. A man with whom I can be truly free of all my embarrassment and fears.

List of 50

1. Is single.

2. Is committed to being and remaining my best friend and is committed to loving me, being with me, enjoying me, and learning about and from me.

3. Is committed to self-responsibility and self-actualization and is actively engaged in improving one's own spiritual, emotional, mental, and personal growth.

4. Understands and accepts my strengths and weaknesses in experience and knowledge and actively, unconditionally, and non-judgmentally engages in helping me grow spiritually, emotionally, mentally and personally and is fully supportive of my personal growth.

5. Daily recognizes and is actively working through and dealing with own issues, past and present, in a self-responsible, open manner.

6. Participates actively in promoting communication using the Communication Model and is committed to at least half an hour of honest open communication each day.

7. Is totally trustworthy, and is open, honest and vulnerable with me and trusts me completely with all secrets, past, present and future.

8. Is brave, loyal, polite, faithful, reliable and patient.

9. Is committed to understanding, learning about and loving my children unconditionally.

10. Is committed to our relationship being second only to the relationships between our children and ourselves.

11. Believes in and employs only constructive criticism and suggestions if asked for and totally accepts and understands that I must make my own choices.

12. Enjoys mutual cuddling, massaging, caressing, touching, tenderness and intimacy.

13. Is diplomatically assertive.

14. Stays in the present when we are together or talks and discusses and explains why if when not in the present.

15. Listens non-judgmentally and understands with detached compassion.

16. Believes in and is committed to responsible drinking and is non-judgmental of the drinking habits of others.

17. Enjoys traveling and meeting new people.

18. Is mid-line extrovert, introvert.

19. Is enthusiastic and positive about life.

20. Enjoys and seeks out learning new things and is committed to interests outside work and home and sharing them with me, and is committed to my having outside interests and sharing them too.

21. Is committed to including me and my children in all areas of their life.

22. Has at least one university degree.

23. Is in a helping/teaching career and enjoys work time as much as playtime.

24. Is committed to understanding, and interested in learning about and from people of different races, religions, cultures, and backgrounds, nonjudgmentally and unconditionally.

25. Is living their Christian faith, and is committed to deepening their spirituality and relationship with God, through accepting and using the good in other religions.

26. Is financially responsible and is committed to saving for the future, as well as enjoying the benefits of money in the present.

27. Is kind and compassionate to all people and understands and is committed to our family having priority over anyone else.

28. Is a smart, safe, experienced driver whom I feel totally safe and secure with when driving.

29. Is actively committed to staying healthy and eats sensibly, exercises regularly, and employs de-stress techniques.

30. Is a good cook and enjoys cooking.

31. Is committed to sharing the household duties 100 percent and enjoys each of us doing more on occasions, should we choose to.

32. Is committed to sharing expenses and will pay/or allow me to pay without keeping track.

33. Keeps their home, car and other possessions clean, orderly, and running smoothly.

34. Has and uses common sense and intuition.

35. Can play a musical instrument fluently and is open to and committed to teaching me to play.

36. Can speak a two or more languages fluently and is open and committed to teaching me.

37. Is technologically savvy and enjoys and is patient with teaching me more about technology.

38. Can speak and write intelligently and creatively.

39. Enjoys conversing on a variety of topics with ease, intelligence, and grace.

40. Has creative intelligence, and encourages creativity in me.

41. Is spontaneous and flexible and also enjoys structure and planning.

42. Is environmentally aware and active in enhancing, preserving and maintaining natural environments and ecosystems.

43. Is a non-smoker, and believes in using traditional western as well as eastern healing methods and uses drugs only for prescriptive purposes and only for healing.

44. Manages time wisely.

45. Peace loving and committed to peaceful surroundings.

46. Has a good sense of humor and enjoys and appreciates my sense of humor.

47. Likes to get up early, and also likes to sleep in on occasion.

48. Likes to dress and look attractive at low cost and will splurge on occasion.

49. Likes a variety of music.

50. Is physically stronger, bigger, and taller than me.

References

Allen, Wayne C. This Endless Moment. Waterloo, Ontario: The Phoenix Centre Press, 2005

----------------- Living Life in Growing Orbits: 52 Weeks to Wholeness. Waterloo, Ontario: The Phoenix Centre Press, 1998

----------------- Half Asleep in the Buddha Hall, Waterloo, Ontario: The Phoenix Centre Press, 2010

Dawkins, Richard. The Selfish Gene. New York: Oxford UP, 1976.

Efran, Jay S., Lukins, Michael D., Lukins, Robert J.. Language, Structure, and Change. New York: W.W. Norton, 1990

Goleman, Daniel. Emotional Intelligence. New York: Bantam, 1995

McKeen, Jock & Wong, Bennet. The Relationship Garden. Gabriola Island, B.C.: PD Publishing, 1996

Peck, M. Scott. The Road Less Traveled. New York: Simon & Schuster, 1978

Schnarch, David. Passionate Marriage. New York: Henry Holt and Company, 1997

Wong, Bennet & McKeen, Jock. The NEW Manual for Life. Gabriola Island, B.C.: PD Publishing, 1998

www.ingramcontent.com/pod-product-compliance
Lightning Source LLC
Chambersburg PA
CBHW050645160426
43194CB00010B/1811